GUIDED BY TRUTH

ENDURING FAITH®
CONFIRMATION JOURNAL

This journal belongs to

____

and I started my journey on

____

Acknowledgments

Thanks be to God for the beautiful work He carries out when His people collaborate in ministry and for all the congregations, church workers, volunteers, and peers who have ever shared in that exercise with me as we consider new approaches to teaching the faith. Special thanks are owed to Pete Jurchen for the inspiration to consider the Six Chief Parts through new perspectives in his book *Timeless Truth*; Lindsey Schmidt and Joel Symmank of Woodbury Lutheran for their field-tested approach to using a journal to pass along the faith and their willingness to share their materials and priceless feedback as we adopted a similar approach; and many at Trinity Lutheran in Klein, Texas, particularly John Cordrey, who helped ensure our journal became a reality.

A special thanks to God is owed as well for those He used to pass on the faith to me throughout my life and those who helped me learn what it means to pass on the faith to others, especially Scott Malme and Hal Toenjes, who taught me so much on my vicarage at Pilgrim Lutheran in Green Bay, Wisconsin, and Pastor David Brighton, who guided my confirmation journey at Mount Calvary Lutheran in Warner Robins, Georgia, and encouraged me to pursue God's calling into pastoral ministry.

May God continue to raise up those who share a passion for both learning about and passing on the central teachings of the Christian faith.

3558 S. Jefferson Avenue, St. Louis, MO 63118-3968
1-800-325-3040 • cph.org

Written by Lee Hopf

Manufactured in China/064570/418096

2 3 4 5 6 7 8 9 10 11 33 32 31 30 29 28 27 26 25 24

Table of Contents

Unit 1

Starting the Journey . . .

NOTES

Imagine going on a hike. This isn't just any hike—it's the most incredible hike you could ever go on.

Imagine passing a river that has some of the toughest rapids in the world, then passing another place that is so calm you can see yourself in the water as you're walking by. Imagine a forest so dense that you can barely see as you walk through, only to later be in another part that is so full of life and light and color that you'll never forget it. Imagine climbing to the top of a mountain and taking in the most beautiful landscapes you have ever seen, only to climb down into a valley and encounter the coolest and deepest caves as you're walking along.

Imagine taking that journey.

Every one of us is on that kind of a journey. It's called life. That journey begins when we're in the womb and will continue until the day that Jesus returns. Sometimes, the journey is thrilling; other times, it seems boring. Sometimes, it seems dark and makes us afraid, while other times, it brings us beauty and meaning beyond what we could have ever imagined.

As we take this journey, we ask ourselves some pretty important questions along the way: What am I supposed to do with the time that I'm given for this journey? Will I make the most of it? Or will I rush through and miss some of the best parts? Will I give up when the journey seems tough? Or will I keep pushing toward the end that we all know is worth it?

You have come to a crucial point in that journey. We call this part of the journey **confirmation**. It's time to grow deeper in this thing you've been given in your Baptism, which is called faith. It's your time. You hear this word *disciple*, and you want it to be a word that describes you. You want to both identify deeply with what it means to be a disciple and own it as part of who you are.

When you come to the end of this leg of the journey, you will publicly confirm both your baptismal faith and your identity as a follower of Christ. And that's no small thing.

This confirmation journal is a tool to help you along the way.

NOTES

1.1 Getting Ready

As you work through this journal, you'll be exploring this Christian faith that was given to you in your Baptism and also why we believe what we do. Just like any good hiker, you'll need a couple of tools to help you along the way:

- ☐ **God's Word—the Bible.** This is no ordinary book. In its words, we find life, and we find a living and active God. This is the most important tool for the journey! We'd all be lost without it.
- ☐ **Luther's Small Catechism.** Sometimes, it's nice to have a guide. The Small Catechism is a summary of what God's Word teaches us about the faith that was given to us in Baptism. When you need a quick reminder, this book is that helpful guide!
- ☐ **Faith Habits.** Along the way, you'll be exposed to the basic habits we share in the Christian life. These habits will help you foster and grow in the faith that was given to you in your Baptism. Just like hikers know they need water to stay strong for the journey, we know these habits keep us spiritually fit.

Question numbers throughout this journal refer to the 2017 edition of *Luther's Small Catechism with Explanation.*

Each page in this journal is an opportunity for you to grow in this faith that you are beginning to claim as your own. While each lesson may be brief, try to keep in mind that the goal isn't to finish the journal quickly. **The goal is to learn and explore your faith.** Remember: no journey worth taking should be rushed. Enjoy it!

While you can use this journal by yourself, the journey will be even more enjoyable and meaningful if you share this journey with those God has placed in your life. Now is your opportunity to engage in conversations of faith with your parents, your guardians, and other adult mentors in your life who want you to continue to grow in this faith God has given to you.

Something else to keep in mind: ***every time you open this journal, find an opportunity to pray before you start.*** Seize every one of those opportunities to pray. Ask God to open your eyes and your heart to what He would have you see and learn. Then take your time with what follows.

Really think through what's being asked in this journal, and you will gain a deeper understanding of each piece of this baptismal faith that you are about to explore. **Take the time to write out your thoughts** rather than scribbling down a few words. It will make the journey all the more valuable by the end.

Finally, as you work through this journal, know that this is *your* journal. Use the margins to write any questions, thoughts, or ***ahas*** that you might have along the way. Talk about your questions with someone at home or at church. Share your ahas! It's exciting when God shows us something we've never thought about before.

As you go on this journey, you'll notice that this journal has been broken down into units for you. At the end of each unit, ask your confirmation leader for the Unit Check-In so that you can share your learning.

This may seem like a lot! But I've got one more piece of advice before you begin your journey: enjoy it. ***It will be worth it.***

NOTES

Read

HEBREWS 11:1; EPHESIANS 2:8–9; 3:17–19

What do these verses say about faith that you might be able to share with someone who has never heard the term *faith*?

Faith is a gift. Why is it helpful for us to remember that God gives us faith rather than thinking that we somehow earn it or come up with it?

Reflect

What do you think is the most important thing Christians should remember about faith?

NOTES

As you start your confirmation journey, what questions do you have about the journey ahead of you?

A friend of yours who doesn't go to church with you hears this word for the first time: *confirmation*. They ask you, "Hey, I know you're doing this thing called confirmation. What is that all about?" What would you tell them?

As you begin this confirmation journey, **write a prayer to God in the space below** thanking Him for this opportunity and asking Him to keep your heart and mind open as you continue forward.

1.2 Where to Go?

As you start reading your catechism, you'll see this question often: **"What does this mean?"** As we take these first steps in the journey, let's start with an easy observation: we are Christians. But the question for us as we begin may be one you haven't wrestled with before: What does it mean to be a Christian?

Imagine that you're in an elevator, and someone steps on with you and sees that you're wearing a shirt with the name *Jesus* on it. The person looks at you kind of excited and says, "I've always wanted to meet a Christian, but I've never had the chance. I'm curious: What does it mean to be a Christian?" In the space below, **write how you would answer them**.

A Christian is . . .

Probably the simplest answer we can give goes something like this: a Christian follows Jesus. Another way you might phrase it could be this: a Christian is someone who believes in Jesus Christ as his or her Savior, Redeemer, and Lord. What did you come up with?

Whenever you go on a journey, part of the preparation has to start with this question: Where are we going? When it comes to this journey we call life, many people really don't know the answer to that. They are left asking the question "Where do we go?" or "How do we even begin to know where to go?"

For us, we can provide a little direction to someone who might feel lost. Think about it: where someone goes depends entirely on what (or who) they're following. **For us, as Christians, we know where we're going because we know *who* we're following. We're following Jesus!** That's why we call ourselves Christians.

Part of this journey will be exploring what this means. What does it mean to follow Jesus? What does it mean to believe in Jesus as my Redeemer and Savior?

NOTES

That will all come. Until then, let's look at some places in Scripture that help us to see the importance of both following Jesus and believing in Him.

Read

JOHN 5:24 AND ROMANS 10:9

What do these verses tell you about believing in Jesus?

What is the most important point to remember from these verses? Why?

JOHN 8:12

What is the promise that Jesus gives to those who follow Him?

How does this promise connect to the gift of faith and believing in Jesus?

JOHN 6:66–68

What reason does Simon Peter give for following Jesus even when many people turned away from Him?

Open your Small Catechism to Questions 1, 4, and 5.

Read through the questions and the verses given. Which of the verses that you read stood out for you the most? Why?

REMEMBER! When you're asked to look at a "Question" in your Small Catechism, it means to read through the question, answer, Bible verses, and notes!

Reflect

What does following Jesus look like? How would you be able to tell if someone followed Jesus just by watching that person for a day?

How would you define *belief* to a first grader? What does it mean for a Christian to believe in Jesus?

Talk to God the Father for a moment in prayer, asking Him for help as you continue to follow Him. Thank Him for the gift of faith that allows you to believe in His Son. If it helps, **write it in the margin**.

NOTES

1.3 We Need a Map

If you want to get to where you're headed, you need to know where you're going. Seems obvious, right? We need a map. We might know *who* we're following now, but it only helps if we see where He's going. So how do we find out?

There are plenty of places to go these days if you want to find information. Years ago, we'd head to the library and search through books to find what we needed to know. Today, someone might simply pull out a phone and head to the internet to find an answer. But what about us? And what about our question that we wrestled with last time? We now have a good definition of what a Christian is, but where do we turn to back up our definition?

Where would you go or who would you talk with to back up your definition of what a Christian is? **Write your answer below.**

I would go . . .

You could ask a friend. You could search the internet. You could turn on the television or even post to social media and ask the world for an answer to the question. When we do that, we'll find hundreds (or millions!) of different answers. Everyone will have an opinion.

So where do we turn?

God is pretty smart. He knows that we need something a little more reliable than social media. So He gave us something that is always reliable, will never steer us in the wrong direction, and will always be the place to go whenever we have a question about life, faith, or any number of things. When we want to know the answer to some of life's questions (such as "What is a Christian?"), look no further than the most reliable source for all of those questions: God's Word.

We'll learn more about God's Word as we continue this journey—we'd be hopeless without it! Until then, just remember: when you find yourself forgetting what it means to be a Christian or you feel like you've lost your way and need a good road map to get you back, turn to the only reliable source to bring you to the right answer. **Turn to God's Word.**

Read

ISAIAH 40:8

Lots of things are temporary, but God's Word isn't. Why is it comforting to know that God's Word remains forever?

1 THESSALONIANS 2:13

What does this verse tell us about what God's Word can do?

How is God's Word different from other sources of information?

NOTES

NOTES

Reflect

What questions do you have up to this point in the journey about confirmation? about faith? about God's Word? **Write your questions below or in the margin**, and challenge yourself to **ask a trusted adult these questions** in the next couple of days.

Why is God's Word a better source of information about what it means to be a Christian than people on social media or the internet?

Before you turn to your next lesson, **write down everything you know** about our "road map" that we call the Bible in the space below. Include anything at all!

1.4 So . . . What Is the Bible?

We've already tackled some big questions in this journey together: What is a Christian? Where do we go when we want to learn what a Christian is? You'll find that **this confirmation journey is really an experience in asking some of life's biggest questions and turning to God and His Word for answers we can truly trust**.

As we continue this journey, be sure to **write down other questions you have along the way**! That way, you'll be able to remember them to ask your parents, guardians, leaders, or pastors later.

While we're asking great questions, let's go ahead and tackle another big question. We now know that God's Word is our road map that helps us find answers to some of life's biggest questions, but what is God's Word? **What is this thing we call the Bible?**

Go ahead and **write down some of your thoughts in the space below**. (Feel free to revisit some of your answers from the end of your last lesson too!)

Those thoughts will be a good starting place! Now, it's time to dig in some more.

NOTES

Consider this question: "What is the Bible?" That can be a big question with a very long answer! So let's simplify the answer into this definition: **The Bible is a record of what God has done throughout history.**

Go ahead and **rewrite that exact definition** in the space below.

Take your time as you write! **Say each word out loud, and write each word slowly.** Every word is important and has significant meaning.

Think about each phrase in that definition:

- ☐ ***The Bible***—The Bible is unique. It's unlike any other book in history. It has many authors and was written over thousands of years. We don't have other "bibles"—there's just one thing we're referring to when we use that word; it's not a bible among many—it's *the* Bible.
- ☐ ***Is a record***—Often, you might hear someone use the word *story* when it comes to what we read in the Bible. What we need to remind one another, however, is that the Bible is a record of **actual events**. These were **real** people and **real** events. The Bible is a very **real** account of **a very real and present God at work in this world**.
- ☐ ***Of what God has done***—As you read the Bible, what you'll find is that God is continually at work with His people. God doesn't stop loving us, and He doesn't stop showing up in the lives of His people. Ultimately, as the Bible shares with us what God has done, **it's also showing us what God continues to do in and through His people—even today!**
- ☐ ***Throughout history***—Think about that word *history*. It's really a good word when we think about the Bible. As we mentioned above, the Bible is a very real account of what God has done—it's history; it's fact. What we can also remember as we think about the Bible as history is that God is ultimately in charge of everything. He's the author of history.

This means that history is really HIS story—it's God at work throughout time.

As you continue to engage with the Bible, remember the incredible work that God did through His people to make it possible for you to hold the book we call the Bible in your hands. Also keep in mind what it is as you read it: it's a record of what God has done throughout history.

Also remember one of the biggest things you learn from the Bible as you read and hear what it says: God isn't done yet. Yes, it may be a record of what God has done in history, but it also shares with us what God continues to do and will do throughout time—but we'll get to that.

Reflect

What's the most important thing for people to know about the Bible?

Why?

What are some of the biggest questions you have about the Bible?

NOTES

Scenario

A friend of yours asks you, "I don't understand why we need the Bible. What do you think?"

How do you answer him or her?

Check out Questions 7 and 9 in your Small Catechism.

Below, **write at least three takeaways** from what you read.

Remember to talk about your journey (that includes your answers to these questions) with your parents/guardians!

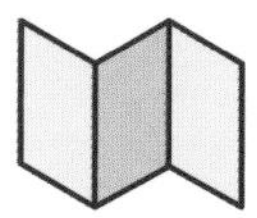

1.5 The Basic Map

NOTES

Before you get buried in the details, it's nice to have a good overview of the journey you're about to go on. It helps to see the basic outline of the map to help you put everything in perspective. If you're taking a road trip to Kentucky, it'd be nice to know what states you're headed through before you start talking about which gas stations you'll stop at along the way. Otherwise, you'll get lost before you get going.

The same is true for the Bible. It's helpful to see the big, overarching picture before we get swallowed up in the details and miss the point.

What's helpful to remember about the Bible is that as it shares with us where we've been and where we're going, it's ultimately reminding us that we're a part of something so much bigger than we could even imagine. One big journey of God with His people. One grand narrative of where we've been and where we will be.

Now, every good story, every good joke, every decent movie, every good paper you write for a class has three main parts: ***a beginning***, ***a middle***, and ***an end***. Eliminate one of those three parts and you've got a pretty quick story (with no middle), a confusing one from the start (with no beginning), or an incomplete one (with no end). When it comes to the bigger picture of the Bible, the same principle applies.

So when we take a look into the Bible—a record of history—we're talking about the beginning, middle, and end of the history of all creation. Sounds pretty daunting, doesn't it? How can we even begin to wrap our minds around that?

Here's the awesome thing: God has already shown us the beginning, middle, and end of this awesome thing we started to explore in our last lesson: the Bible. That's right! The Bible lays out for us where everything started, how it continued, and where it will end up.

This picture will help remind you how simple the big picture of God's master plan really is.

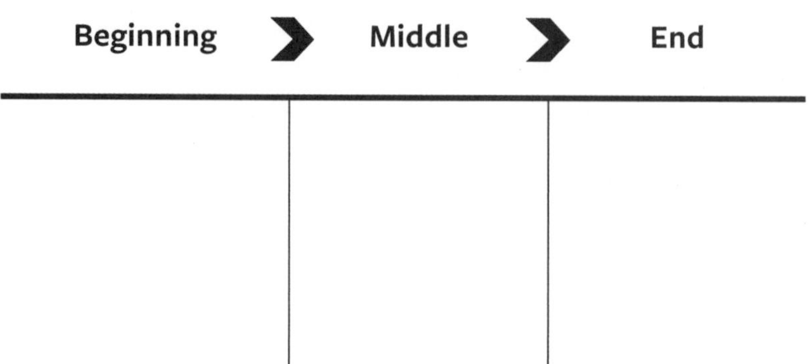

So where do you think it all starts? The beginning, of course! The very first verse of the Bible says, "In the beginning, God created the heavens and the earth." Pretty simple, right? In the "Beginning" column above, **draw the earth from God's perspective** after He created all things. Start by drawing a circle and then fill in the earth with the continents and oceans.

Now reflect on what it must have been like to be there on that day. It was perfect. In fact, do you remember the words used in Genesis to describe the world after God created it? **Take a look at Genesis 1:31 and fill in the following**: "God saw everything that He had made, and behold, it was ____________________." (Keep your Bible open!)

So what happened after creation? If you aren't as familiar with what we refer to as "the fall," go ahead and brush up on it by reading Genesis 3. **Make some notes in the space below** about what we refer to when we say "the fall":

Sin entered into this world because of the temptation of Adam and Eve. God's perfect creation had fallen in the sense that it was no longer perfect because of sin's presence in the world. But God made a promise!

In Genesis 3:15, God promised that He would send an answer to the problem of sin in the world. That verse assured God's people that one day, God would send someone who would be an answer to sin and who would bring about the restoration of His creation. That's when we come to the middle of God's big picture of history.

For the middle section, we can label this "Jesus." Jesus was God's answer to the problem of sin in this world. Jesus is the one who would restore the world to the way God had designed it. In the "Middle" column of your diagram, **draw what comes to mind when you think of Jesus**. Maybe you'll draw a cross or an empty tomb. Maybe you'll draw Jesus doing one of His miracles. Whatever it is, use the space to illustrate this middle point of the big picture of what God is doing and has done in this world.

Now reflect on what you know about Jesus and what He did. **Write some thoughts below**.

You might be saying to yourself, "Wait a minute! If Jesus came to restore things to the way God designed them, then why is there still sin and brokenness in this world?" Exactly! If we cut the big picture short with the life and ministry of Jesus, it's like telling a story without the ending. When we think to ourselves, "Wait! This doesn't seem finished!" we're right on track.

There's more to the picture.

Throughout Jesus' ministry, He reminds His followers that there is a day coming that is pretty important. Some refer to it as "Judgment Day" because it's the day when Jesus will return in glory to "judge the living and the dead," as we say in the Apostles' Creed. As Christians, we refer to it in plenty of ways! Some of our favorites are "the Day of Resurrection" or "the Day when Christ returns." The Book of Revelation in the Bible paints an interesting picture of that day as an ultimate final battle between God and His enemies: sin, death, and the devil.

While many see that day as one to be afraid of, as Christians, we can look at that day with joy and hope in our hearts! That day is the day when Jesus will **restore all things** to the way they were meant to be once and for all. The fire that is mentioned in Revelation is one

NOTES

NOTES

that is meant to purify and clean, much like you clean a stick in the fire when you've been roasting marshmallows. It's all about bringing the restoration that God promised from the very beginning.

What words or thoughts come to mind when you think about the day when Jesus will return? **Write them in the space below.**

In the "End" column of your drawing, **draw the earth again** like you did in the first drawing— go ahead and draw your circle, draw the continents, and fill in the oceans. Now **draw a cleansing fire or a burst** (like you see on packages that say "NEW!") **around the earth** to show the restoration and cleansing that God will do to restore all things to how they once were.

That's the BIG PICTURE we get when we read God's Word.

It's as simple as remembering the beginning, the middle, and the end. Leave one out, and things get a little confusing. Bring them all together, and you've got **a great perspective to see what God has done, is doing, and will do in the future**!

Reflect

How might knowing the bigger perspective of the beginning, middle, and end help someone to make more sense of the world around us?

What advice would you give to someone who is afraid of the day when Jesus will return?

What new things did you learn from this lesson?

NOTES

NOTES

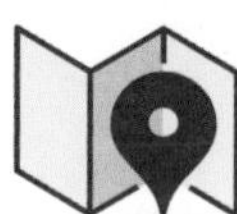

1.6 A Fuller Map

Now that we've got the basic overview of our map down (the beginning, middle, and end), it might be helpful to get a fuller picture of the journey from start to finish.

The Bible lays out for us how God has interacted with His people since the beginning, but have you ever sat down to map it all out?

Sometimes when we read the Bible or hear it read in church, it can be a little confusing because we really don't have what we call "context" for what's going on. We don't really know the bigger picture or how each event connects to the others. We've heard about Moses, but was that before or after Abraham? It makes a difference! We know that Isaiah talked about Jesus, but wasn't he a prophet well before Jesus? Without context, the Bible can become confusing pretty quickly.

Reminding ourselves of a fuller picture of the Bible can help us in those times. It's helpful when we read to remember the context—that is, what came before and what comes after. It helps us to see where it all fits in the big picture of what God has done and was doing at the time.

For this lesson, we've got a (mostly) blank map numbered 1 through 12 on pages 24–25. We'll describe each step along the way, and you will complete the map by following the instructions in this lesson.

Let's start with an easy one:

1. ***Genesis***—It's best to start at the beginning. This time, let's use the word *Genesis*, which is a word that means "beginning" but is also the name of the first book in the Bible. This leg of the journey is full of a lot of people and events that you're probably familiar with: Adam and Eve, Cain and Abel, Noah and the flood, Abraham and Isaac, Jacob and his twelve sons, and so on. For this section on your map, **write "Genesis," and draw a world** similar to the one you drew in the previous lesson.

2. ***The Exodus***—After Genesis comes the "Exodus." It might seem like we're just going in order of the books of the Bible, but this is a reminder that the exodus is more than just a book of the Bible—it's a significant event for God's people. The exodus refers to when God used a man named Moses to take God's

people from Egypt into the Promised Land. For this section of your map, you'll notice a treasure map. At the top of the map, it says "Promised Land." **Draw a dotted line with an arrow pointing to the X.** The people travel to the place promised by God. The other big thing God's people get through the great exodus is the Ten Commandments. Go ahead and **write the number *10* on the tablets** to signify the Ten Commandments. **Write "The Exodus" next to the drawings**, and you're good to go to the next one.

3. *The Cycle of the Judges*—Once God's people make it to the Promised Land, they start to ask God for rulers—specifically, they ask for a king. The one thing they're forgetting (of course) is that God is King! Even so, God gives them rulers called judges. During this time, it seems like the Israelites fall into the same pattern over and over again: Israel serves the Lord, then they fall into sin and idolatry; eventually they get conquered, and only then do they cry out to God; then God raises up a judge, Israel is delivered, and they return to serving the Lord—BUT then they fall back into sin and idolatry. That's why we call this section the "Cycle of the Judges." For your map, **write the phrase "Cycle of the Judges" in the middle of the circle of arrows** to remind you of what's going on during this time.

4. *The Kings and the Prophets*—Finally, God gives the people what they ask for: a king. Remember that Israel already has a king (God is King), so this can't be good for them in the end (and it isn't!). During this point in Israel's history, God appoints kings. And alongside of them, He establishes a group called prophets. What's the main job of a prophet? To proclaim God's Word both to His people and to Israel's king. On your map, you'll notice a megaphone and crown. **Write the phrase "Kings and Prophets" near the drawings, then write the phrase "God's Word" on the megaphone** to remind you of what a prophet's role would have been.

5. *A Kingdom Divided*—Here's the thing about humans: we like power. Turns out the kings of Israel liked power too. So much so that at one point the kingdom of Israel split into two kingdoms (the Northern Kingdom, called "Israel," and the Southern Kingdom, which they called "Judah"). Israel was in trouble the moment they asked for kings, but this division is

God's Journey with His People

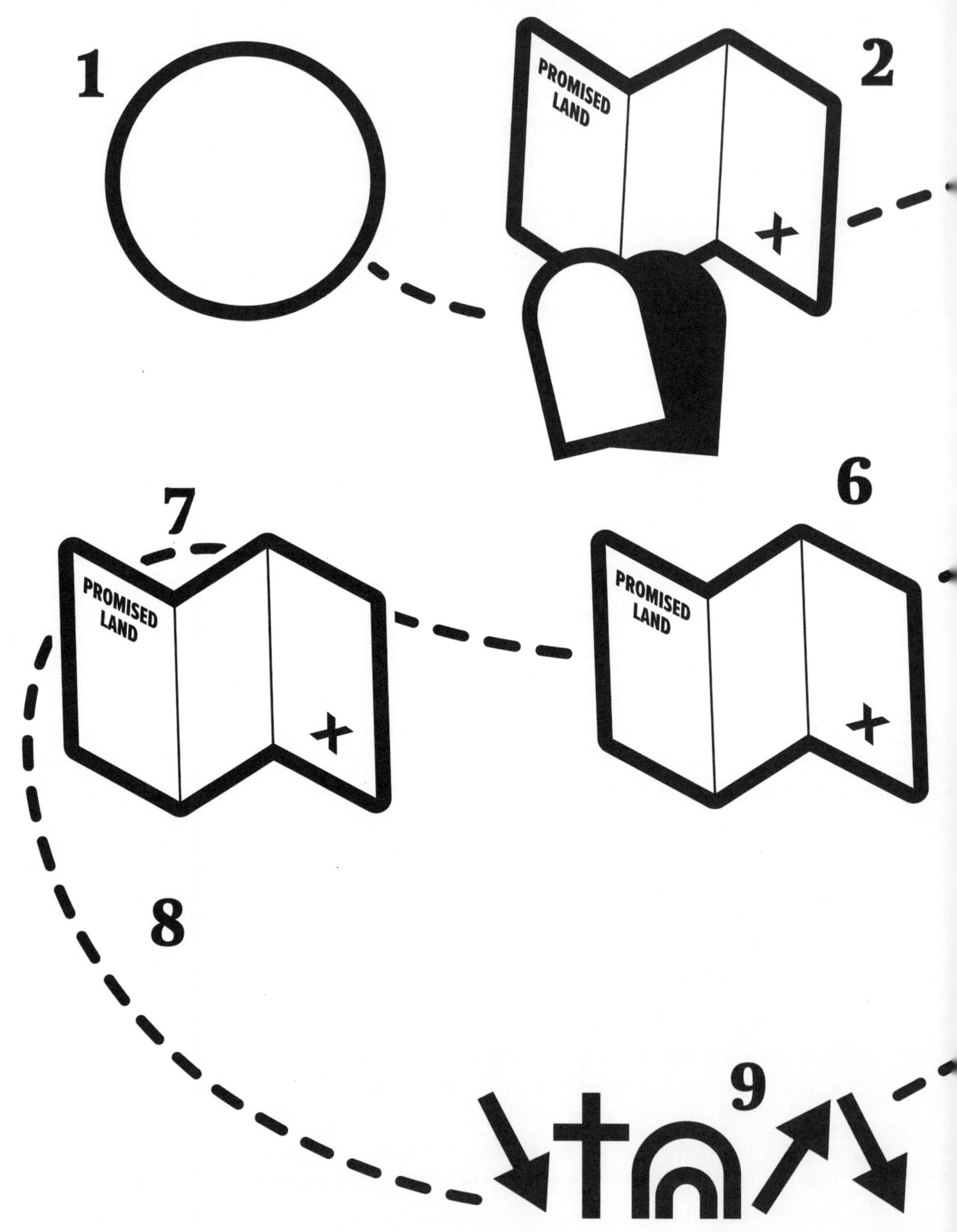

3
4
5
11
10
12

NOTES

certainly a sign that something bad is about to happen to Israel. For your map, **draw a jagged line through the throne to signify Israel's division, and write the phrase "A Kingdom Divided."**

6. ***The Exile***—Those kings eventually turn to idolatry and start looking like other nations. If there's one thing God doesn't like, it's idolatry. By this point, God has had enough of it. He allows foreign countries to come in and take over the Israelites and remove them from the Promised Land. This is the most difficult part of Israel's history. You'll notice the Promised Land treasure map again. **Draw arrows all around pointing away from the X** to remind you of how the Israelites were taken out of Israel during this time. **Write "Exile" somewhere near this picture.**

7. ***The Return***—Thankfully, the exile was not the end of the Israelites' journey with God. Eventually, God brought the Israelites back to the Promised Land. This time, things are different because everything has been destroyed. It's during this time that the Israelites rebuild—but it still never feels the same for them. Before the exile, God dwelled with His people in a very real way. Now, God seems to be absent. In the meantime, God's people wait for the promised restoration of Israel. For this section, **write "The Return" and draw arrows pointing back to the X on the map** to remind you of this time for God's people.

8. ***The Silence***—This section might seem pretty strange on your map—the space is just blank! That's because during this time we don't have any record of what's going on with God or with His people (not in the Bible, at least!). For four hundred years, all we have is silence. As you can see from your map, God won't be silent for long! For this section of your map, **write "The Silence" along the dotted line that goes from 8 to 9** to remind you of this time in Israel's history.

9. ***Jesus***—We've covered a lot of ground in this section we're calling the "beginning." Now our map leads us to the "middle" of God's journey with His people. For this section, you'll see five little symbols that show us the full picture of what Jesus has done and will do in the future. The goal is to remember this phrase: **He came, He died, He rose** (it's an empty tomb!),

He ascended, and He's coming back. Use the space in the margin to draw the five symbols you already see on your map. Write the words connected to each symbol next to them. For this section of your map, **write "Jesus" below those five symbols on the map**.

10. *The Early Church*—After Jesus ascends, He sends His promised Holy Spirit to the apostles, and the Church spreads and grows in dramatic ways! This is recorded in the Book of Acts. As you'll see from your map, the symbol shows arrows all around the world. That's because Jesus' followers are doing exactly that during this time—they are going to all parts of the world, telling everyone they can about Jesus. It's a great reminder for us of what our role in this world is too! For this part of your map, **write "The Early Church" near the symbol**.

11. *The Modern Church*—After the apostles went out into the world spreading the Good News about Jesus' death and resurrection, the Church started establishing itself in permanent buildings so people could regularly come together for worship. As time moved on, God's Word spread throughout the world more frequently through book form. We see this especially during the time of the printing press and the efforts of the Reformation. God's Word is now in a format that is accessible for people in their own languages! For this stop, we've got an open Bible to symbolize this time for the Church. On your map, **write "The Modern Church" next to that Bible** to help you remember this period in history.

12. *Jesus Returns*—You guessed it! We already covered the beginning and the middle, so we might as well fill in the end. For this section on your map, **draw the same earth with fire or sunburst around it that you did in the last lesson and write "Jesus Returns" next to it**.

NOTES

NOTES

And that's a wrap! You've got a fuller picture of the history that the Bible covers. Now when you hear someone read from the Bible in class, at home, in Bible study, or in a sermon, ask yourself, "What part of the bigger picture is this happening in?" It will help you to think a little deeper about what God had done up to that point and what God would continue to do after.

1.7 Our Compass

When you look at a map, one of the first things you want to find is the compass. In order to make sense of the map in the first place, you need to be holding it the right way. A map isn't very useful when it's upside down. Without a compass, you'll probably wind up holding your map the wrong way, and you may end up going in the complete opposite direction from where you meant to go. No one wants to do that.

Something similar could be said when it comes to our map, the Bible. How do we know we're "holding our map" correctly? How do we know we're reading our Bible from the right perspective? How can we assure ourselves that we aren't just getting ourselves lost and heading in the complete opposite direction? Well, just like when you look at a map, we see what our compass is telling us.

Now, that might sound funny. The Bible doesn't have a compass in the literal way that a map does. Instead, our compass is found in the answer to this question: What is the point of the Bible? **Write your thoughts in the space below.** Why do we have the Bible? What's the thing that the whole Bible points to?

Go ahead and open up your Small Catechism to Questions 6 and 8.

Read through the questions, answers, verses, and notes, and then come back and summarize the point of the Bible in one word in the space below.

The central message of the Bible (in one word) is . . .

NOTES

What is the word you chose? Did you write "Jesus"? Seems too simple, right? Isn't that the right answer for any question you get asked in church? Well, think about it: we need a compass, something that helps us to see if we're going in the right direction as we're navigating this map we call the Bible. In a sense, you could say that the Bible is both our map *and* our compass. Why? Because it points us to Jesus.

The key is Jesus. How do we know we are reading the Bible correctly? We're reading it right when it's pointing us to Jesus—what He says, what He's done, what He continues to do, and what He will do when He returns. If it isn't pointing us to Him, then we might need to find our compass and get back on the trail.

Reflect

Describe a time when you started heading down the wrong path or making a poor decision because you were following the wrong thing.

Whenever you lose your way (maybe you make a poor decision or find yourself not acting like yourself), who or what helps you get back on track?

Read

JOHN 5:31–47

Who or what testifies about Jesus?

- ☐ v. 33: ______________________
- ☐ v. 36: ______________________
- ☐ v. 37: ______________________
- ☐ v. 39: ______________________

Why does Jesus say that if they believed Moses, they would believe Him?

Sometimes, we read the Scriptures but we don't always see Jesus when we do (see v. 39). We read the Bible but forget that it is showing us more about Jesus. **Write a short prayer in the space below**, asking for guidance to help you see Jesus as you read His Word.

Sometimes when we read the Bible, we end up looking more for ourselves and what we want in the Scriptures rather than looking for Jesus. How might this cause a problem for us and steer us in the wrong direction?

Reread the Small Catechism Questions 6 and 8.

Pick one of the verses in this part of the Small Catechism to show that the Bible points to Jesus. Which did you pick? **Write it here.**

NOTES

NOTES

1.8 Law and Gospel

Ever been taught the difference between a political and a physical map? The concept is actually pretty simple. The two types of maps have different purposes. A political map shows us boundaries, like where one county starts and another ends. Meanwhile, a physical map shows us the natural features of whatever region we're looking at. If you want to know where mountain ranges are, a political map isn't going to do you much good. However, if you need to know the boundaries of your county, it works just fine!

The Bible works in a similar way (but all in one map). It functions in two primary ways. We call them the two great doctrines (a fancy word for teachings) of the Bible: Law and Gospel.

Unlike the different purposes of a map, when we talk about Law and Gospel, it isn't just about being able to decipher what is Law and what is Gospel. It's more about what the Word of God does to us as we receive it. The Holy Spirit (and we'll get to Him!) works both Law and Gospel in us as we read the Word. Our hope as we start to explore Law and Gospel is that we'll come to see how God uses both to create and nurture faith in us, which leads to eternal life.

One way to remember the ways Law and Gospel work is to remember the letters *SOS*.

Turn to Questions 10 and 11 in your Small Catechism.

Complete the chart based on what you read.

LAW	GOSPEL
What does the Law teach?	What does the Gospel teach?
Shows our ________ (SOS)	Shows our ________ (SOS)
To whom must the Law be proclaimed?	To whom must the Gospel be proclaimed?

Three passages are listed under Question 11:

- ☐ Romans 3:20
- ☐ John 6:63
- ☐ Romans 1:16

Write "L" or "G" next to those passage references labeling them as Law or Gospel.

Here's the thing to remember about Law and Gospel: **we need both!** Sometimes, we might need to have the Law working on us, while other times we need what only the Gospel can give. We need to hear the Law to learn what we are to do and not to do (think Ten Commandments). Meanwhile, we also need the Gospel to know what Jesus has done for us. On the one hand, we need to hear the Law because it helps us come face-to-face with the reality of our sin (and we become sorry for our sins). On the other hand, we need to hear the Gospel because it gives us comfort in our sorrow.

Reflect

Describe a time when you did something wrong but, instead of being punished, you were forgiven.

How did that feel? Why do you think it felt that way?

NOTES

Scenarios

Your friend Thomas is in an ongoing fight with his parents. They have given him a curfew of midnight on Friday and Saturday nights, but he always breaks it—sometimes by a little, sometimes by a lot, but he always breaks it. They've grounded him, taken away his cell phone, taken away all kinds of privileges, but Thomas doesn't care. He says the rule is stupid and so are his parents.

Does Thomas need to hear Law or Gospel? What would you say to him?

A different friend, Megan, has messed up. Megan told a secret about April that she had promised to keep to herself. As soon as Megan said it, April walked around the corner and everyone looked at her and started laughing. Megan saw the hurt in April's eyes and ran off, ashamed about what she had done. For the whole next week, Megan wouldn't go anywhere near April because she was so ashamed. Finally one night, April texted Megan, but Megan wouldn't even read it. When she finally did, it said, "I know what you did: you told the story about me. I'm embarrassed that people know my secret now. But you are my friend, and I don't want this to come between us. I can forgive you, but please don't avoid me anymore." Megan doesn't know what to do. How could April ever forgive her?

Does Megan need to hear Law or Gospel? What would you say to her?

1.9 Faith Habits for the Journey

In our very first lesson, we talked about some important tools you'll need for this journey we call life. The most important was the one we've spent a lot of time talking about in this unit: God's Word—the Bible. We'd be lost without our map! The second was one that you've been using throughout this first unit as well (and it's a summary of what God lays out for us in the Bible). That would be Luther's Small Catechism. I hope you've started to appreciate how helpful both of those will be for the journey!

As we start to wrap up our first unit, we want to bring back the last tool we mentioned in that introduction to the journey. Here's what we said:

> ***Faith Habits.*** **Along the way, you'll be exposed to the basic habits we share in the Christian life. These habits will help you foster and grow in the faith that was given to you in your Baptism. Just like hikers know they need water to stay strong for the journey, we know these habits keep us spiritually fit.**

The first of the seven faith habits we want to explore in this lesson is one that will be vital for the journey:

FAITH HABIT #1: REQUEST THE SPIRIT.

Let's keep it simple. **We'd be lost without the Spirit.**

From what we see in Scripture, the key difference between those with faith and those without it is the presence of God's Spirit within His people. **And faith makes all the difference in the world!** Faith is what guarantees us the promise of eternal life. Faith is what works in us when we engage God's Word and see the promises He gives to us in and through the death and resurrection of Jesus Christ.

That's why the outpouring of the Holy Spirit into the Church (that is, into God's people) through His Word and through our Baptism is so important. We have this promise: God is not only with us, but He also dwells within us.

NOTES

This first faith habit will be one that we use over and over again in our daily lives (just like the rest of the faith habits that we'll learn!). The first habit is learning to talk to our triune God and **requesting that His Spirit be with us**.

When you engage God's Word or enter into God's house for worship, pray that the Spirit would work in your life. This prayer will help you to focus on worship and the study of His Word, drowning out all the distractions and helping you to remember that God has promised to work through His Word. Thank Him for this vibrant and living gift that He gives to all His children. Through His Word and through the Sacraments (such as Baptism), the Holy Spirit gives and nurtures faith. As this prayer for the Spirit becomes a habit (like breathing!), you will start to see your faith mature even more.

Reflect

Describe a time when you needed help in order to understand something. Whom did you turn to? Why did you turn to that person?

How does it make you feel to pray, asking that the Spirit would work in your life? Why do you think you feel that way?

Read

LUKE 11:9–13

What promise does Jesus guarantee in verse 13?

Notice that gifts Jesus talks about are of the Spirit. He's not talking about worldly wants but spiritual ones (like love, joy, peace, patience, and so on).

You had a little bit of practice in writing a prayer that you could say any time you open up God's Word in Lesson 7. Now it's time for you to write another short prayer that you will use every time you open this journal moving forward.

- ☐ **Write a prayer in the space below**, asking God to let His Spirit work in your life as you engage with His Word. Thank Him for this gift and the assurance that He has promised to work through His Word.
- ☐ **Write this prayer on a note card** that you can use as a bookmark for your journal! It will help you remember to pray each time you open it up.

NOTES

Remember to request the Spirit.

NOTES

1.10 Another Faith Habit for the Journey

As Christians, we understand that each of these faith habits are equally important for our spiritual lives. In the same way an athlete or a musician develops healthy habits so that they can be successful as they perform, so do we develop these faith habits as we continue to grow in our walk with God.

With that, we've got one more faith habit for you before we conclude Unit 1:

FAITH HABIT #2: READ AND REPEAT THE WORD OF GOD.

Throughout this unit, we've talked about how important God's Word is for our lives. God's Word, through the Holy Spirit, points us to Jesus, works within us both Law and Gospel, and gives to us this gift called **faith**, which leads to eternal life! Nothing else in all creation can do something like that. God's Word is powerful.

But . . . it can't do much when it's sitting on a shelf.

Did you know that you could get in the best shape of your life by subscribing to an exercise app or buying a healthy eating plan book? Well, not quite. You see, exercise videos aren't helpful if you never watch and follow along, and a book about healthy eating isn't very helpful if you never open it.

The same can be said for God's Word. We need it. We know we need it. Too often, however, we're not in it. **It's time for a change.**

If someone wants to get stronger, they probably won't do it by doing one push-up. Instead, they'll need to do multiple push-ups—and not just once but over the course of months and years.

For us, we need to engage the Word of God on a regular basis. Reading the Bible every once in a while isn't going to get your faith into shape. It's going to take reading and repeating God's Word—repetition—in order to see real results.

Reflect

What are some things in your life that require good habits? Maybe it's a sport, a musical instrument, or some other talent.

What would happen if you stopped spending time on the habits you needed for those activities?

If we know God's Word nurtures our lives, why do you think it's so hard for people to stay plugged into it on a regular basis?

What advice would you give to someone who is struggling to stay in God's Word and to develop a healthy habit of reading and repeating it?

NOTES

Read

ISAIAH 55:10–11

Then read it again. And again.

What promise does God give about His Word in these verses?

PSALM 1

Read it more than once.

What does the writer of this psalm say is the source of the man's happiness (v. 2)?

This psalm uses metaphorical language. It says the man in the psalm is like a tree. What is God's Word like (v. 3)?

You have completed Unit 1.

Complete your Unit Check-In.

Unit 2

Who Am I?

NOTES

Ever heard of an identity crisis? An identity crisis is what happens when a person loses sight of who she is, or—perhaps—when a person feels like he had no sense of who he ever was in the first place. An identity crisis can be triggered by a number of factors, but most often follows a time when some sort of major change occurs in the person's life.

Imagine being a great athlete who has a career-ending injury or a pianist who is diagnosed with arthritis in both hands at a young age. Those sorts of situations could cause quite the identity crisis. Who is an athlete without her sport? Who is the musician without his ability to play anymore? They might think to themselves in those moments: I'm no one.

Here's the thing: life is FULL of major changes. Sometimes, people you love die. Sometimes, your family situation changes and there's nothing you can do about it. Sometimes, you end up going to a new school with new people in a new place and feel like you have to start all over.

So how do you not lose sight of who you are when that time comes? Is there a way to prevent an identity crisis before it even begins? Is it possible that who you are is actually something that never changes even when the rest of the world around you seems to be constantly changing?

That's what we get to explore in Unit 2. **God has something to say about your identity—and it never changes.**

And that's good news! Crisis averted.

NOTES

2.1 Your Identity

Let's go ahead and take a stab at the question we're focusing on for this unit: **Who are you?**

How would you answer the question if someone just came up to you and asked, "Who are you?" **Use the space below to describe yourself.** Feel free to draw pictures in the margin too!

Think about what you said above. How much of that stuff has a chance of changing in your lifetime?

If you mentioned family, chances are, in thirty years or so, your family might look different than it does now. If you mentioned a sport or a hobby, you may not still be doing those things ten years from now, or you may have found new interests. So what is it about you that is something that will never change?

Let's turn to Scripture to find out. It's exciting when God shows us something we've never thought about before.

Read

PSALM 139:13–14

David wrote these words, but what David says is true for you too. What do these verses tell you about yourself?

1 JOHN 3:1

Who (or what!) does this verse say that you are?

GENESIS 1:26–27

What do these verses say about you?

Here are some of the takeaways from those verses:

- ☐ **You are first and foremost a creation of God.** He made you. He knit you together before you were born into this world. He knows you better than anyone else. And that will never change.
- ☐ **You are His child.** No one can take that away from you! How great is God's love for you? Enough that He would pour out His love over you as His child through His Word and in your Baptism through Jesus Christ. And that, too, will never change.
- ☐ **You were made in the image of God, according to His likeness.** You were created to reflect the God who made you, who loves you, and who provides for you. Guess what? You guessed it! That will never change either.

That's your identity. That is who you are. But what about God's plan for you? What is your calling?

NOTES

Reflect

If I were to tell you that God has the same plan for each and every one of us, what would you guess that purpose is? **Write your guess in the space below.**

We find our answer to God's plan and purpose for us in a place you might not expect: the Ten Commandments. **This is where we learn the truth that God does have a plan for us as His human creatures and where we learn about God's Law**. That means the fundamental answer to the question "What is my purpose?"—one of life's biggest questions—is found in the Ten Commandments.

Write a prayer in this space asking God to help remind you that you were created by Him for a purpose.

When you reflect on the Ten Commandments, you learn that you are God's human creature, created on purpose, for a purpose: **to love God and love your neighbor.**

2.2 God's Top Ten List

What are some of the rules in your house? **Write them in the box to the right.** Write at least three, but feel free to write as many as you can.

RULES IN OUR HOUSE:

Choose one of those rules (circle it), then write an explanation of why you think your family has that rule:

Why do we make rules in the first place?

We are part of God's family. We are all His children, we are all His creation. That means we're all living under the same "house" (so to speak), and that means . . . house rules.

Open up your Small Catechism and read Questions 15 and 16.

Read

MATTHEW 22:36–40

Jesus gives us a summary of all of the "house rules" for God's family. **Write the summary in your own words below.**

NOTES

When we look at the Ten Commandments, we can see Jesus' summary of all of God's Law as well. We call this the "Two Tables of the Law."

Fill in the hearts after you've read the Matthew passage.

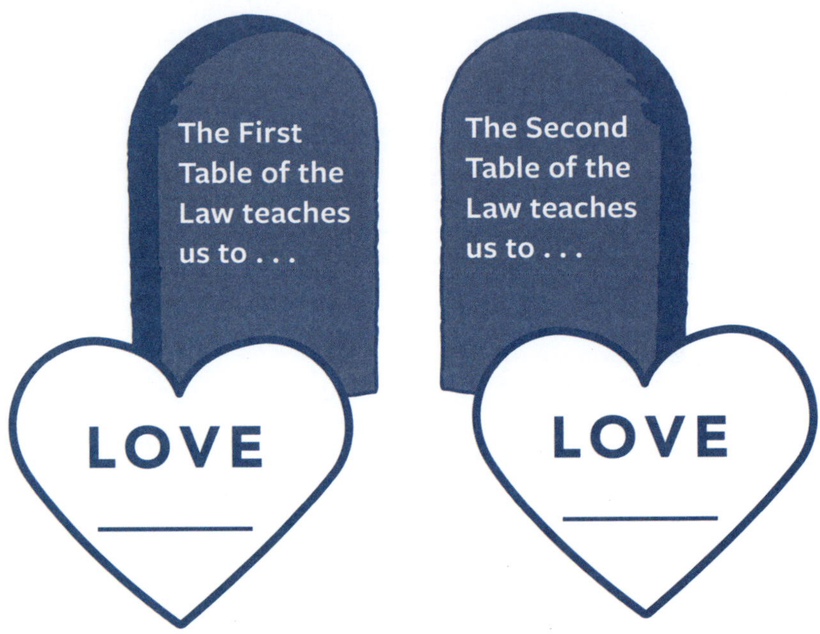

God's Law helps us to see our purpose: **to love Him and love others.** But have you ever wondered how we got God's Law?

Open up your Small Catechism and read Question 17.

Then, **in your own words, write in the blanks below how we come to know God's Law**.

First, God wrote it ______________________.
(See Romans 2:14–16 for a refresher!)

Then, God wrote it ______________________.
(See Exodus 20:1–17 for a reminder!)

NOTES

It might seem a little strange that God's Law has been written onto the hearts of all people, especially since not all people believe in Jesus. But remember, we are talking about God's Law! That is, we're talking about God's will for the lives of all people.

Note: This is referring to God's moral laws (which tell us what is right and what is wrong), not the ceremonial laws of the Old Testament (like what to eat and when to pray).

What would be one thing that everyone knows is wrong, even non-Christians? **Write down an example in the space below.**

See! God's Law has been placed on the hearts of all people. God created all people with a conscience, a sense of what is right and what is wrong, to help guide us in our behavior so that we might do His will.

Reflect

Think of a time when you felt guilty because of something you did. Why did you feel guilty? What is it that helped you to know that what you did was wrong? Maybe you don't want to include a lot of detail—that's understandable. Write as much as you feel like you can.

NOTES

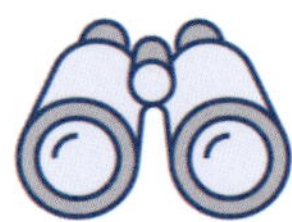

2.3 But Why?

Why? Why did God give us the Law in the first place? Life would have been a lot simpler without it, right?

Did you know this was an important question for Early Christians to wrestle with too? In his Letter to the Galatians, Paul has to remind the people that God's promise of salvation was given through faith (not through the Law). He shows the Galatians that we can see this in Scripture because God gave the promise of faith to all people through Abraham 430 years before He gave the Law through Moses (Galatians 3:17). That's a long time! The Law didn't remove or take the place of the promise of faith (which leads to salvation); it was given for an entirely different purpose.

You see, God's people spent so many years with the Law by the time that Jesus came, **they forgot the whole reason why the Law was given in the first place**. Somewhere along the way, they started believing that the Law was given so that they could earn salvation (even though there's no way any of us could earn that—because of our sinful natures; we'll talk about that in Unit 5).

That's why this question is an important one for us to remember. We don't want to trick ourselves into thinking that following God's Law is somehow earning us salvation. Rather, we need to remind ourselves of why God gave it to us in the first place.

So, why did God give us the Law? The answer is as easy as 1, 2, 3. We find our answer in what we call **the three uses of the Law**.

Open your Small Catechism to Questions 18 and 19 to complete the next page.

The Three Uses of the Law

1. The Law is like a ______________.
God's Law helps keep order in the world. It leads people to do what is right and avoid doing wrong. The Law helps us avoid dangers by showing us the consequences that can happen when we do bad things.

2. The Law is like a ______________.
God's Law shows us our sinful selves and condemns our sin. When we look at God's Law, we realize that we could never keep it perfectly, and we often break it.

3. The Law is like a ______________.
God's Law guides Christians to live God-pleasing lives through our thoughts, words, and actions. The more time we spend with God's Word and His Law, the more we are reminded how He designed us to live.

Remembering why God gave us His Law in the first place can be very helpful when we think about why we do not want to sin. It's not because we're trying to earn God's love—we already have that! We follow the Law because God loves us. He loves us and wants what is best for us. The Law of God helps keep us in check, convicts us when we've strayed, and guides us in the way we should live.

NOTES

Scenario

Your friend Damien stops you at school and says, "I saw you didn't come to that party this weekend. Figured it was because of the alcohol. What's up with that? Still trying to impress God by following all of His rules?"

How would you respond to Damien?

2.4 Loving God

When Jesus began His ministry, the leaders of God's people listed six hundred and thirteen laws that they were expected to follow. Can you imagine? **Six hundred and thirteen!** How do you even begin to keep track? God gave Ten Commandments, but the leaders added way more.

The greatest skill of a rabbi (a teacher) would have been to narrow the Law down to as few as possible that would summarize all the rest. Even if you could get it from six hundred and thirteen down to one hundred, that would have been impressive. So imagine how hard it might be if you had to figure out which one was the most important law of them all!

At one point, Jesus is asked exactly that question. Some Pharisees, wanting to test Him, asked Jesus what the greatest commandment is. Here is how it went down:

> **But when the Pharisees heard that He had silenced the Sadducees, they gathered together. And one of them, a lawyer, asked Him a question to test Him. "Teacher, which is the great commandment in the Law?" And He said to him, "You shall love the Lord your God with all your heart and with all your soul and with all your mind. This is the great and first commandment."**
> **Matthew 22:34–38**

NOTES

Love God. Out of six hundred and thirteen laws, Jesus narrows it down to one and says, "This is the most important commandment."

You are about to explore the First Table of the Law (the first three commandments from God's "Top Ten List"). They are all about **what it means to love God**. Before you do, let's reflect on what it means to love God in the first place.

Jesus was quoting from the Old Testament when He responded to the Pharisee. Take a moment to explore the passage He was quoting.

Read

DEUTERONOMY 6:1–9

What do you feel is the main point of what God says here?

Which verse is Jesus quoting?

If you could use only one word to summarize what God is asking from you in this verse, which would you choose?

Why did you choose that word?

Reflect

Take a moment to think about what it means to love God with all your heart, with all your soul, and with all your strength. Here's the one word that comes to mind for me when I think of what God expects from us: *everything*.

Use the questions below to reflect on what it means to love God according to Deuteronomy 6:5. Feel free to draw pictures, but **be sure to write words to remind you of what they mean**.

What do you think it means to love God with all your heart?

What do you think it means to love God with all your soul?

Talk to your parents/guardians about your answers once you've finished.

What do you think it means to love God with all your strength?

NOTES

2.5 First for a Reason

Imagine that somewhere in the world, there was a room with a single chair sitting in the middle of the room with the sign "Throne of _______________'s Life" resting above it. (Go ahead and write your first name in that blank.) Whatever sat on that throne (or whatever was placed onto that throne) would be the sole thing that ruled your life. Like a king rules a kingdom, whatever that thing sitting on your throne wanted, it would get. Whatever it said, you'd do. It's king. That's how it works.

Now imagine that every person had a throne like that.

What are some things you think people have sitting on their thrones? What are things that you see "ruling" people's lives? What things do people treat like kings—things that control their desires, thoughts, words, and actions? **List them in the space below** (draw pictures if you'd like).

Even though none of us have a literal "throne" of our lives, we do have things that we allow to control us. These are the things we put first. These are the things that consume most of our time and our thoughts. If something goes wrong or we lose whatever it is that's sitting on the throne, we think our world is falling apart. Maybe it's money. It can even be family. Often, it's our stuff (our material possessions) or the image we want others to see on social media. Here's the reality: **that throne was only made for one person to sit on it. That person is God.**

When we look at the Ten Commandments, here's something to keep in mind: God put the First Commandment first for a reason. Without God on the throne of our lives, we're in trouble.

Open your Small Catechism and turn to the section on the First Commandment. Fill in the blanks below.

The First Commandment

__________ shall have __________ other __________.

What does this mean?

We should __________, __________, and __________ in __________ above __________ things.

Read the rest of this section of the Small Catechism on the First Commandment (including all questions, verses, and notes). **Make notes in the margin** to remind yourself what sticks with you most from this section. Any good questions? Anything you want to remember to go back to? Write a page number or a quote to help you remember.

NOTES

Scenarios

As you read each of the following scenarios, ask yourself, "What is sitting on the throne of this person's life?" Put another way, "What is this person fearing, loving, and trusting above all other things?"

You return from Christmas break to find one of your closest friends, Timothy, looking upset. When you ask Timothy about it, you find out that he didn't get much for Christmas this year. On top of losing most everything in the flood, his dad was recently laid off. Timothy says to you, "It's just not worth it any more. I'm a nobody now. How can anyone like me? How will a girl ever want to date me if I don't have nice things? We don't have money like everyone else around here. We probably just need to move—it's too embarrassing to stay around here. My life is over."

What do you think is sitting on Timothy's throne? Why do you think that?

Understanding what you've learned about the First Commandment, what would you say to Timothy?

You find your friend Sarah crying as she's waiting to be picked up from school. You find out that Sarah's mom just called her and told her that Sarah's grandpa just died. She wanted Sarah to know that before she got picked up. Sarah is hurt because her grandpa was the only one that held the family together and under control. Now that her grandpa is dead, the family will never be the same again. Sarah's entire world, she says, is over. Sarah then looks at you and says, "You go to church—why would God take away the only thing that was constant in my family?"

What do you think is sitting on Sarah's throne? Why do you think that?

Thinking about what you've learned about the First Commandment, what would you say to Sarah?

You are a sophomore in high school. Your friend Angelina just texted you and said that her world is over. When you ask her what happened, she replies, "Maalik broke up with me." Angelina and Maalik have dated since eighth grade and seemed to be the perfect couple. They went everywhere together! They have all the same friends. Angelina has had a rough time lately even before the break up. Maalik was her whole world. She texts you, "He was the only one who could ever make me smile." It's clear that she found her happiness in Maalik.

What do you think is sitting on Angelina's throne? Why do you think that?

How could what you've learned about the First Commandment help you to talk with your friend Angelina?

NOTES

NOTES

Reflect

Take a moment to look back over everything you've learned about the First Commandment (it's first for a reason!). **Write a prayer in the space below asking God to help you keep Him first.** Ask Him to help you to fear, love, and trust in Him above all things, especially in areas where you feel like you're struggling to do that.

Do I Have an Idol?

The First Commandment is all about idolatry (and God's not a fan). Idolatry is when you place anything but God in the throne of your life. When you do that, that thing becomes what you fear, love, and trust in more than God. It becomes its own "god."

Now is the time for self-evaluation to see if you might have an area of your life that is turning into an idol. **Rate the following statements on a scale of 1 to 5 (5 = always, 3 = sometimes, 1 = never).**

1. ____ I need to have power or influence over others.
2. ____ I need to experience a level of comfort or a particular quality of life (pool, big house, nice car, etc.).
3. ____ I need to control my life.
4. ____ I desire people to lean on me or need me.
5. ____ I like it when I'm completely free from obligations or responsibilities to take care of someone.
6. ____ I'm only happy when I'm getting a lot done.
7. ____ I feel valued if I'm noticed for my accomplishments.
8. ____ I feel important because I have wealth.
9. ____ I prefer to be independent of organized religion, and I prefer living by self-made rules.
10. ____ My race or culture (being a Texan or a Husker fan) is superior.
11. ____ It's important for me to be one of the "cool kids."
12. ____ I often look for a girlfriend or boyfriend and believe it is important for me to have that kind of relationship.
13. ____ I believe my political or social views are best, and I'm unwilling to listen to people who think differently.
14. ____ I need to look good or have a particular body.
15. ____ I think that what I post on social media has to be perfect, and I want as many likes as I can get.
16. ____ If I were to be without my smart device for a day, that would be the worst day of my life.

NOTES

To understand your results, use the key on the reverse side of this page.

NOTES

Take a look back at your answers on the previous page. **Make sure you were honest before you keep going!** This is meant for you to help identify potential idols so that you can start working on them now—rather than being hurt by them later.

Here's how you should read your answers on the previous page:

1: That is not an idol in your life.

2: Sometimes it tempts you, but it's not an idol.

3: Sometimes, this is an idol in your life. Time to reflect.

4 or 5: Consider talking to a mentor, parent, or pastor about strategies to start taking this idol off your throne.

Below is the answer key for what may be sitting on your throne (an idol in your life) based on your evaluation. For example, "Power Idolatry" would mean that your desire to have power would be sitting on your throne.

1. Power Idolatry
2. Comfort Idolatry
3. Control Idolatry
4. Needed Idolatry
5. Independence Idolatry
6. Work Idolatry
7. Achievement Idolatry
8. Materialism Idolatry
9. Self Idolatry
10. Cultural Idolatry
11. Popularity Idolatry
12. Relationship Idolatry
13. Ideology Idolatry
14. Self-Image Idolatry
15. Social Media Idolatry
16. Smart Device Idolatry

2.6 Carry It Well

You're helping at a food bank, and someone asks you to help carry their bag out to the car for them. You look over, and there's a paper bag sitting on the counter. How do you carry it? Do you grab the handles? Or do you grab it from the bottom?

It all depends on what's inside. If what's inside isn't all that important, or if it doesn't weigh a lot, then you can probably grab the handles and not think twice about it. However, if what's inside is heavy or fragile or important, then you'll probably want to grab it from the bottom of the bag just to make sure it's protected.

Open your Small Catechism and turn to the section on the Second Commandment. Fill in the blanks below.

The Second Commandment

You shall not ______________ the ______________ of the LORD ______________ God.

What does this mean?

We should ______________ and ______________ God so that we do not ______________, ______________, use satanic arts, ______________, or ______________ by His name, but ______________ upon it in every ______________, pray, ______________, and give ______________.

Let's put God's name in that paper bag on the counter. How do you carry it? When we treat God's name with the respect it deserves, it's like we're carrying the bag from the bottom. We know it's important, so we take care of it. When we throw it around without care and without respect, we might as well be swinging that bag around by its handles—even though something very valuable is inside.

Explore the rest of the Small Catechism on the Second Commandment, and make notes in the margin like you did for the First Commandment. Take your time!

NOTES

Reflect

What are some bad ways you've heard your friends use God's name? These would be times when people say "God" or "Jesus" when they aren't praying, praising, or giving thanks to Him. **Write them in the space below.**

Put an "X" through each of the phrases above. These are all the ways that people carry God's name without care or respect.

What are some areas where you need help respecting God's name?

Think about opportunities in your life where you could use God's name more often (in an appropriate and respectable way).

- ☐ At home
- ☐ At school
- ☐ At church
- ☐ With friends

We have the opportunity to carry God's name with us everywhere we go. God spoke His name over us in our Baptism, and He speaks it over us each week as we go to church and are forgiven. It is a powerful name! We see Jesus' apostles use His name to cast out demons as they go out in ministry.

For this reason, it is our desire to carry God's name well. We carry it with respect and love, we use it often—especially in prayer and praise—and we want others to hear it and come to know the promise that can be found in Jesus.

As you read the rest of the section on the Second Commandment in your Small Catechism, make your notes in the margin!

NOTES

NOTES

2.7 True Rest

The word *Sabbath* is from the Hebrew word *shabbath*, which means "rest." The Third Commandment is all about rest.

Open your Small Catechism and turn to the section on the Third Commandment. Fill in the blanks below.

The Third Commandment

____________________ the ____________________ day by ____________________ it ____________________.

What does this mean?

We should ____________ and ____________ God so that we do not ____________ preaching and His ____________, but hold it ____________ and ____________ hear and ________ it.

What picture comes to mind when you think about rest? Maybe you think about a pillow, a fluffy bed, a comfy couch, or getting as much sleep as you possibly can. You wouldn't be alone in thinking that way. How do you know when someone is well rested?

Think about it this way: true rest can only be known by its result. When you're truly rested, you are energized and ready for a new day or the next task. Here's what we learn from Scripture: **our rest comes from God.** More specifically, we find rest when we are fed by God's Word. It rejuvenates, energizes, and helps us be ready for the work God has in store for us each day and in each moment.

If we know that God's Word is where we find rest, let's also think about all of the places where we can be fed by God's Word. What are all the ways and places you hear or engage with God's Word? **Write them in the margin.**

Each of those places are opportunities to love God—which is what these first three commandments are all about! When we skip out on opportunities to hear or engage with God's Word, we're neglecting opportunities to love God.

Read

LUKE 10:38–42

Like Martha, we can become distracted and anxious about many other things that really don't matter in the end. When those times come, remember Jesus' words:

> **Martha, Martha, you are anxious and troubled about many things, but one thing is necessary.**
> **Luke 10:41–42**

It's important to keep God's Word before us, whether it be in worship together, in Bible study, or during personal or family devotions. God's Word shows us our sin, points us to our Savior, offers forgiveness for our sins, strengthens our faith, defends us from the devil, and encourages and equips us to live lives of faith.

In other words, when the world tires you out, God's Word gives you rest. True rest.

NOTES

Scenarios

You're a sophomore in high school. You invite one of your classmates, Blake, to church. He says, "No thanks. I used to do the church thing. It was pretty boring. Besides, I don't have to go to church to be a Christian."

Keeping in mind what you've learned about the Third Commandment, how would you respond to Blake?

List three great things God does for His people through worship. (Hint: See Question 52 in the catechism.)

1.

2.

3.

You're a senior in high school, and you offer your little brother, Jeremy, a ride to youth group. He says, "I don't want to go! It's stupid and not any fun. All they do is Bible stuff. It's lame. It's not like I need to learn any more, anyway. I learned enough growing up."

Knowing what you know now about the Third Commandment, what do you say to Jeremy?

2.8 Loving Others

Remember Lesson 2.4? Jesus wasn't done after He said to the Pharisee, "This is the great and first commandment." He had one more way He wanted to sum up the Commandments—you might say this is the "second half" of God's Law:

> **And a second is like it: You shall love your neighbor as yourself. On these two commandments depend all the Law and the Prophets. Matthew 22:39–40**

Just like that, Jesus sums up all those laws in two: **love God and love your neighbor**. Jesus points to Deuteronomy 6:5 and Leviticus 19:18 (never let anyone tell you nothing good comes from Leviticus!) to summarize all of God's Law.

You've explored what it means to love God; now, it's time for you to take a look at that second half. You are about to explore what we call the Second Table of the Law (the last seven commandments from God's "Top Ten List"). They are all about what it means to love others. **Before you look at the individual commandments, this one-page lesson is an opportunity for you to reflect on what it means to love others.**

During Jesus' ministry, an expert in the law was asking himself the same question. He was curious what it meant to be a neighbor and, in turn, love his neighbor as himself.

Read

LUKE 10:25–37

Now is your time to reflect. **Fill the margins of this page** with ways you can love your neighbor, or remind yourself what it means to be a neighbor. Ask yourself, "What does it mean for me to love my neighbor as myself? What does it mean for me to be a neighbor?"

NOTES

2.9 That It May Go Well . . .

Did you know that God placed into each and every one of our lives people who are meant to represent Him? You might be tempted to think it's your pastors. Sure, pastors are God's representatives, but we're talking about all people (not just those who go to church). By design, every single person on earth was meant to have certain people who would be God's representatives in their lives.

Have you guessed who it is yet? Parents. Yes, not everyone has parents, but that was God's design for His creation—that every one of us would have people in our lives who would take care of us, protect us, love us, know us, and guide us in the same way that God does for all of us.

So as we turn the corner to the Second Table of the Law (where we learn what it means to love our neighbor), who does God place first? Our parents. He places parents right next to Him on the "Top Ten List."

Open your Small Catechism and turn to the section on the Fourth Commandment. Fill in the blanks below.

The Fourth Commandment

______________ your father and mother.

What does this mean?

We should ______________ and ______________ God so that we do not ______________ or ______________ our parents and other ______________, but honor them, serve and ______________ them, love and ______________ them.

There's something really interesting about the Fourth Commandment—something entirely different than the other nine. It's the first one that includes a promise attached to it.

Open up to Ephesians 6:3 (which is quoting Exodus 20:12) **and write the promise in the margin.**

You may have noticed something interesting in the "What does this mean?" section in the catechism this time around. When reflecting on what God's Word says, Martin Luther (who put together the Small Catechism) saw that God was not only referring to parents in the Fourth Commandment but also to all authorities that God has placed in our lives. Without parents or authorities, this world would be in chaos.

Below, you will see several kinds of authorities God uses to carry out His plan, purpose, and order for His creation. **Read the verses associated with each and then answer the questions.**

NOTES

THE PROMISE GOD ATTACHES TO THE FOURTH COMMANDMENT IS . . .

GOD GIVES AUTHORITY	GOD'S WILL
Parents Ephesians 6:1–4	What does God expect of parents? children?
Pastors 1 Timothy 3:1–7	What does God expect of pastors? people?
Teachers Proverbs 3:1–2	What is the benefit of honoring teachers?
Employers Ephesians 6:5–8	How do we honor God by honoring employers?
Government Officials Romans 13:5–7	What does God expect of governments? people?

NOTES

Scenario

Your older cousin, Alaina, is frustrated. She says, "I can make my own decisions now! Why do I need a curfew? What right do they have to tell me that I can't go on this trip with my friends? Why do they care where I go to college next year? I wish they would just butt out and let me do my own thing."

In light of what you learned about the Fourth Commandment, what do you say?

You have the opportunity to honor whomever God has placed into your life as an authority every day. **Write a few ideas down below** on how you could honor a parent or guardian tomorrow. Maybe you write a thank-you letter or do an extra chore. Your choice!

Explore the rest of the Small Catechism on the Fourth Commandment, and make notes in the margin about what stands out to you.

2.10 Always Seek to Help

Open your Small Catechism and turn to the section on the Fifth Commandment. Fill in the blanks below.

The Fifth Commandment

You shall not ______________.

What does this mean?

We should ______________ and ________ God so that we do not ______________ or ________ our neighbor in his body, but __________ and support him in ___________ physical need.

When you first read the Fifth Commandment, you might be tempted to say something like this: "Finally! One I know I haven't broken."

Upon closer inspection in Scripture, however, we find out that it's a lot easier to break than we first thought. This commandment isn't simply about not taking a life (which is definitely an important piece to it!). **It's about honoring life every chance we can.**

What do you think it means to "honor life"? **Write your thoughts in the margin.**

Honoring someone's life is about respecting others at all times. This goes for all people. People who are different than you, people who you don't get along with, people who might even be considered your enemies. God calls us to honor every one of their lives through the Fifth Commandment for this reason:

> **Every person created by God is worthy of respect and dignity.**

Take another look at the "What does this mean?" answer for this commandment. The Fifth Commandment calls you to always seek ways to help and do everything that you can to avoid causing harm—and not just physically.

NOTES

Brainstorm ways that you can avoid causing harm and ways that you can help others and jot down your ideas below.

WAYS TO AVOID CAUSING HARM	WAYS TO HELP AND SUPPORT

God's hope for you as His creation is that you would use your words, actions, and opportunities to help others at all times and to avoid causing hurt or harm by the things that you say or do, or choose not to do. When we cause hurt or harm to our neighbor, it breaks the Fifth Commandment.

Read

MATTHEW 5:21–26

If the Fifth Commandment didn't seem hard enough, Jesus adds something else to the list that we need to be aware of that is right up there with murder.

What does Jesus equate to murder in verse 22?

In what ways is being angry similar to murder? Think about when you've been angry at someone. How was it similar?

Reflect

Bullying is pretty prevalent today. When you think about it, it's probably the most common way the Fifth Commandment is broken. We may do or say things because we think they are funny, when in reality they cause our neighbor harm and devalue his or her life.

What's the most hurtful comment you've ever heard someone say to someone else? How did you feel when they said it?

If you have ever been a victim of bullying, please reach out to an adult for help. You may be affected in ways that are not apparent at the moment.

Brainstorm ways you can support your neighbor. **Write ideas in the margin.**

Scenario

You're outside at school in a group of about ten people. Your friend Jamie says to this guy, "Get out of here, Luke, no one cares about you. You wear stupid clothes, you have ugly shoes, and I have no idea how you look at that miserable face each morning. You should really just kill yourself." Other students laugh. Some don't know how to respond, so they do and say nothing. The bell rings, and you all walk inside.

Keeping the Fifth Commandment in mind, how do you respond to Jamie? to Luke?

NOTES

Think of someone you know who needs to know that his or her life is valuable. Maybe it's someone you have bullied. Maybe it's someone you know who has been bullied or abused. **Take this time to encourage this person through a note or a text.**

Explore the rest of the Small Catechism on the Fifth Commandment, and make notes about what stands out to you. There are a lot of good questions, answers, and verses about life issues in there!

2.11 The Goal Is Holiness

As you look through the Scriptures, God makes something abundantly clear: He is holy; He expects and calls His people to be holy as well.

But what does it mean to be holy? Biblically speaking, it means something like this: **to be set apart**. Another way to phrase it might be "completely different" or "unlike anything else."

It's like if you tried to come up with the best athlete of all time. How would you begin to narrow down the list? By looking at who stands out. Who, as they say, separated themselves from the pack? Who was entirely different?

So what does it mean for us to be holy? It means that God expects us to be set apart for His purpose. Here are just a few examples from Scripture where God makes it clear that He expects us to be holy:

> **It is written, "You shall be holy, for I am holy."**
> **1 Peter 1:16**

> **I appeal to you therefore, brothers, by the mercies of God, to present your bodies as a living sacrifice, holy and acceptable to God, which is your spiritual worship.**
> **Romans 12:1**

> **Since we have these promises, beloved, let us cleanse ourselves from every defilement of body and spirit, bringing holiness to completion in the fear of God.**
> **2 Corinthians 7:1**

> **For this is the will of God, your sanctification.**
> **1 Thessalonians 4:3**

In this lesson, you have the opportunity to reflect on the meaning behind the Sixth Commandment. As you do, remember that God's purpose in giving this commandment to His people reaches beyond simply being faithful in marriage. God's desire for each one of us is to be holy—set apart for His purpose.

What you'll find as you explore the meaning of the Sixth Commandment is that the goal is not as simple as "don't cheat once

NOTES

you're married" (even though that is important)—God certainly appreciates and expects faithfulness and detests unfaithfulness. Rather, the goal is holiness. **The goal is for you to be set apart.**

Open your Small Catechism and turn to the section on the Sixth Commandment. Fill in the blanks below.

The Sixth Commandment

You shall not commit ________________.

What does this mean?

We should ____________ and ____________ God so that we lead a ________________ pure and decent life in what we ____________ and __________, and husband and wife __________ and ______________ each other.

Explore the rest of the Small Catechism on the Sixth Commandment, and make notes in the margin about what stands out to you. There are a lot of good questions, answers, and verses! Topics include living together, divorce, pornography, same-sex marriage, sexual identity, and singleness.

Read

MARK 10:6–9

Remember, this is Jesus talking about marriage.

Who does Jesus say enters into marriage (vv. 6–7)?

What happens in marriage (v. 8)?

How long has this been God's design for marriage (v. 6)?

Reflect

God gave us rules to protect us, bless us, and keep us healthy. This goes for sex and marriage too. **Complete the chart below** by describing how following or breaking God's rules about marriage and sex can affect us. **Ask a parent if you need help!**

EFFECTS OF *FOLLOWING* GOD'S RULES ABOUT SEX AND MARRIAGE ON . . .	**EFFECTS OF *BREAKING* GOD'S RULES ABOUT SEX AND MARRIAGE ON . . .**
our bodies	our bodies
our minds	our minds
our spiritual lives	our spiritual lives

NOTES

NOTES

2.12 Protect Their Stuff . . .

Open your Small Catechism and turn to the section on the Seventh Commandment. Fill in the blanks below.

The Seventh Commandment

You shall not ______________________________ .

What does this mean?

We should ____________ ***and*** ____________ ***God so that we do not*** ____________ ***our neighbor's*** ____________ ***or possessions, or get them in any*** ____________ ***way, but help him to improve and*** ____________ ***his possessions and income.***

At first glance, this commandment seems pretty straightforward: just don't take people's stuff. It applies to big things like cars but also little things like copyrighted material (like illegally downloading music or movies). Before we brush it off as being as simple as not taking someone else's things, however, let's unpack the deeper meaning behind this commandment.

Look a little bit closer at this commandment: we're not being told simply not to take other people's things; we're also expected to **help our neighbors protect and even improve their things**.

In the Second Table of the Law (Commandments 4–10), we're not allowed to simply avoid doing the wrong things and keep to ourselves. As we engage God's Word, we see that He is making it clear that **we also have a responsibility to those around us** when we honor these commandments. Looking at the Seventh Commandment, our responsibility is to build up, look out for, and protect our neighbor's belongings. We aren't being called to simply avoid taking their stuff, we're also called to respect, protect, and help them with their stuff.

Explore the rest of the Small Catechism on the Seventh Commandment, and make notes in the margin about what stands out to you.

Reflect

"This commandment is about whether or not I trust God to provide everything I need." Agree or disagree? Why?

What are some things that people steal? What do you think motivates people to steal those things?

Read

LUKE 19:1–10

In what way had Zacchaeus broken the Seventh Commandment?

In what way did Zacchaeus say he would honor it?

NOTES

Scenarios

Jack, your friend since kindergarten, starts bragging to you about all the new apps he downloaded on his phone. You notice that many of them aren't free apps and you say, "Wow. You must get a pretty good allowance." He laughs and says, "Please. I just use my parents' credit card. They don't know the difference. It's only a few dollars here and there." The reality hits you: Jack is stealing from his parents.

How do you respond?

You live next door to a single mom, Ainsley. One night you hear her outside crying on the phone, "They won't listen to me! I have made every payment, and I've got the proof. There must be a mistake in their system, but I'm just another single mom to them. There's nothing I can do. They're demanding another payment, and they're threatening to evict us."

What might you or your family be able to do for Ainsley?

2.13 . . . and Their Reputation

It's no secret: it's hard to honor the Eighth Commandment. In this commandment, God calls us to respect our neighbor's reputation. This means we have to say "no" to gossip, talking about people behind their backs, talking poorly about people in general, and lying. It's a lot to say "no" to in our world.

For some reason, it's harder to keep ourselves from lying or saying something bad about someone than it is to keep ourselves from murdering or stealing. How crazy is that? Maybe it's because murdering and stealing happen outside of ourselves, with our hands, but lying and slander start within the heart and eventually make their way to our mouths.

The apostle James saw this back in his day too. James compared the tongue to a small flame that ignites a forest fire (see James 3:1–12). Sometimes, one little piece of gossip from our mouths turns into a great force that burns down a person's reputation, or one little joke ends up ruining a longtime friendship. What starts out as harmless ultimately causes some of the greatest destruction.

Open your Small Catechism and turn to the section on the Eighth Commandment. Fill in the blanks below.

The Eighth Commandment

You shall not give ________ testimony against your neighbor.

What does this mean?

We should ______________ and ________ God so that we do not tell ________ about our neighbor, betray him, ______________ him, or hurt his ________________, but ______________ him, speak _______ of him, and explain ______________ in the ____________ way.

NOTES

So whatever you wish that others would do to you, do also to them, for this is the Law and the Prophets. Matthew 7:12

Start seeing every person you encounter as someone who is loved by God and worthy of respect at all times and in all places. That's who they are. When you do, you'll find that it's a lot easier to honor this command and protect their reputation.

Read

MATTHEW 18:15–20

Jesus gives us three steps for dealing with a problem with someone else. Write them here.

Reflect

What does it mean to have a good reputation?

How does it get damaged?

Can it be restored? If yes, how? If no, why not?

2.14 The Secret to Being Content

Open your Small Catechism and turn to the section on the Ninth and Tenth Commandments. Fill in the blanks below.

The Ninth Commandment

You shall not ________________ your neighbor's __________ .

What does this mean?

We should ____________ and _____________ God so that we do not ________________ to get our neighbor's ______________________ or ________, or get it in a way which only appears __________, but help and be of service to him in _____________ it.

The Tenth Commandment

You shall not ________________ your neighbor's __________, or his ______________________, his ox or donkey, or ________________ that _____________ to your neighbor.

What does this mean?

We should ____________ and _______ God so that we do not ________________ or ____________________ our neighbor's wife, workers, or animals, or turn them _________________him, but urge them to ________ and do their ______.

God is showing us that we have a heart condition. By showing us what we ought not to do, He's also pointing out the things that you sometimes want to do. This time, He's asking, **"Are you content with what I have given you?"**

God isn't saying it's bad to want something. God encourages us to be on the lookout for His blessings and all that He provides.

NOTES

Rather, God is warning that sometimes wanting turns into coveting. Sometimes our desires become sinful.

When you look at what you have, do you compare it to what others have? Do you find yourself thinking, "I wish I had more stuff—better stuff—like everybody else?" You might be coveting. Like the Seventh Commandment, these two commandments point us back to all of God's blessings in our lives. They remind us to say, **"God has given me all I have and will provide for all of my needs."**

The person who is able to say these things finds out **what it truly means to be content**.

Reflect

Do you think God promises to give us everything we need or everything we want? Why do you think that?

What are some reasons people are not content with what God has given them?

"Not being content with what you have is like telling God that His blessings are not enough." Agree or disagree? Why?

Read

PHILIPPIANS 4:11–13

Where did Paul find the strength to be content? What was the secret?

Unit 2 Reflection

In the Ten Commandments, God gives you a picture of who you are or—better yet—who He has designed you to be:

Someone who loves God and loves your neighbor.

Whenever you want to discover what it means to love God and love your neighbor, simply turn to His Word. When you do, He also helps you to identify who your neighbor is that you are meant to love.

Your neighbor is the same as mine: it's every person that God has created and placed on this planet. Even the person who doesn't look like you, think like you, talk like you, treat others like you do, believe like you do, or see the world the way you do is your neighbor. And God calls you to love them.

And He also calls you to love Him.

In this unit, we've answered one of life's biggest questions: Who am I? In the next unit, we'll turn our attention to the "big guy upstairs" as we ask the next question: Who is God?

Before we do, take a moment to **write your biggest takeaways** from your time spent with the Ten Commandments and wrestling with this question: "Who am I?"

Fill up the space on this page with what you've learned!

NOTES

You have completed Unit 2.

Complete your Unit Check-In.

NOTES

Unit 3

Who Is God?

NOTES

Your friend notices your shirt. The front says, "God is good." You've never thought much about it. With a confused look, your friend says, "It says 'God is good,' but I'm not sure I know what that means. I mean . . . who—or what—is God?"

If you're like most of us, the answer might not be coming to you as quickly as you thought it would. The question itself might make your head hurt if you think about it too long. It seems like a simple enough question, but for some reason, God is more difficult to describe now that the question is out there.

You might be tempted to respond with something like, "Well . . . He's God!" Then you think to yourself, "Now where do I go from here?" Maybe you say things like, "He's all powerful," "He's just," "He's good," or "He's eternal." Yet even those words don't seem to measure up. All of a sudden, it starts sounding like you're describing the next big superhero or some mixture of all the Avengers rolled up into one.

So what do you do?

This unit is all about helping you wrap your mind around the answer to this question. What you will find is that it really is much simpler than we often try to make it. How do you start to describe the God we serve? By telling what He has done.

Once you come to appreciate what God has done, you come to discover who He is.

The Early Church saw the need to answer this question too. They summarized all of Scripture in such a way that one could quickly describe what God had done—and, in turn, who God is. We call this statement **the Apostles' Creed.**

NOTES

3.1 The Apostles' Creed

In this unit, you will be learning more about the Apostles' Creed as it answers the question that we started with: Who is God? As you begin learning about the Creed, there are a few important things to remember:

- ☐ When we use the word *apostles*, we're referring to the original twelve disciples (minus Judas Iscariot) and Paul, who became one later (Acts 9).
- ☐ The Apostles' Creed is so named not because it was written by the apostles but because it is a summary of their teachings and witness (which we see for ourselves in Scripture).
- ☐ *Creed* is a word we get from the Latin word ***credo***, which means "**I believe**." For this reason, all creeds start with those two words, and we define a creed as simply "a statement of belief."
- ☐ We recognize three creeds to be appropriate summaries of the Bible: the Apostles' Creed, the Nicene Creed, and the Athanasian Creed. All were written at different times, but all are faithful summaries of the Bible and what God has done in history.

When you think about the purpose of the Apostles' Creed, keep in mind the question it answers: Who is God? Also remember the best way to answer that question: we can know who God is by what He's done.

With that, when you look at the words of the Apostles' Creed, you'll notice that it is divided into three parts. We call those the three "articles" of the Apostles' Creed (think of them like paragraphs or stanzas). Each article describes a person of the Trinity (a word that we'll talk about in our next lesson) and His work:

- ☐ The **First Article** talks about the **Father** and His work of **creation**.

- ☐ The **Second Article** talks about the **Son** and His work of **salvation**.
- ☐ The **Third Article** talks about the **Holy Spirit** and His work of **sanctification**.

We'll unpack all of these things throughout this unit. For now, remember that the Creed is simply a summary of what we believe through faith (and it lines up completely with what the Bible teaches): that God created the world, redeemed the world, and sustains His people in faith. Understanding who God is doesn't have to be complicated. It's as simple as reminding yourself of what God has done.

Reflect

Why is it important to have a simple, clear way to state our faith like we do in the Apostles' Creed?

Why is it important that we let the Bible and the Apostles' Creed explain who God is rather than coming up with our own explanation?

"What you believe influences the choices you make." Agree or disagree? Why?

How might people live if they don't believe there is a God?

How might they live if they do believe there is a God?

NOTES

NOTES

Some people say that it doesn't matter what you believe and that all beliefs are equally valid. What do you think?

Read

JOHN 14:6; 3:16

According to these verses, why does what you believe matter?

Scenario

Your friend Safiya doesn't go to a church that uses the Apostles' Creed in church like we do. She seems to have a problem with it. She says to you, "I just don't understand why you need anything but the Bible. Why do you need a creed anyway? All we need is the Bible."

How might you respond to Safiya?

3.2 The Holy Trinity

NOTES

As we've covered so far in this unit, the best way to answer the question "Who is God?" is by responding with what He has done. Who is God? He's the one who created the world, redeemed the world, and sustains His people in faith. As we describe what God has done, we come to discover who He is.

Don't fret if that isn't completely satisfying your need for an answer. God also gives us another acceptable answer to that question in Scripture. When we ask, "Who is God?" we can also respond with confidence:

> **God is Father, Son, and Holy Spirit.**

That might seem strange—and that's okay. Why do we refer to God as Father, Son, and Holy Spirit? Because that's how He has revealed Himself to us. After Jesus' resurrection and immediately before His ascension, Jesus says to His disciples:

> **Go therefore and make disciples of all nations, baptizing them in the name of the Father and of the Son and of the Holy Spirit. Matthew 28:19**

Couple that with another incredibly important verse for God's people:

> **Hear, O Israel: The Lord our God, the Lord is One. Deuteronomy 6:4**

So God is one. And yet God is three.

This is where we get the phrases *Holy Trinity* and *triune God*. These are both phrases that are meant to communicate this "three-in-one" reality about God that is recorded in Scripture. God has revealed Himself as being One but has also revealed Himself as Father, Son, and Holy Spirit.

There's a reason why the Trinity is often referred to as the "greatest mystery of the Christian faith." Human understanding cannot completely comprehend it because we are limited; we aren't God. While it doesn't make complete sense to us, that

NOTES

sort of makes sense too. How? Because God is God and we are not. God is simultaneously comprehensible (through what He has done) and a mystery.

To illustrate this: Have you ever tried to imagine what God must look like? It's difficult to do. On the one hand, we can see God through the work He has done (and continues to do through His people). On the other hand, how do you even begin to illustrate someone who is eternal and immeasurable? Artists throughout the centuries have tried, but every illustration can only come so close.

The same can be said when we try to illustrate the concept of the Trinity. Sometimes, the Trinity is compared to fire. Fire has three parts—flame, light, and heat—but it's all just one thing: fire. Other times, you may have heard God compared to an apple, which has skin, flesh, and seeds but is still just an apple. These all seem to come close—because they start to make sense of something so mysterious—but they also fall short because each person of the Trinity is fully God, not just one piece or attribute of Him.

That's why at some point in the history of God's people, someone developed the drawing you see below:

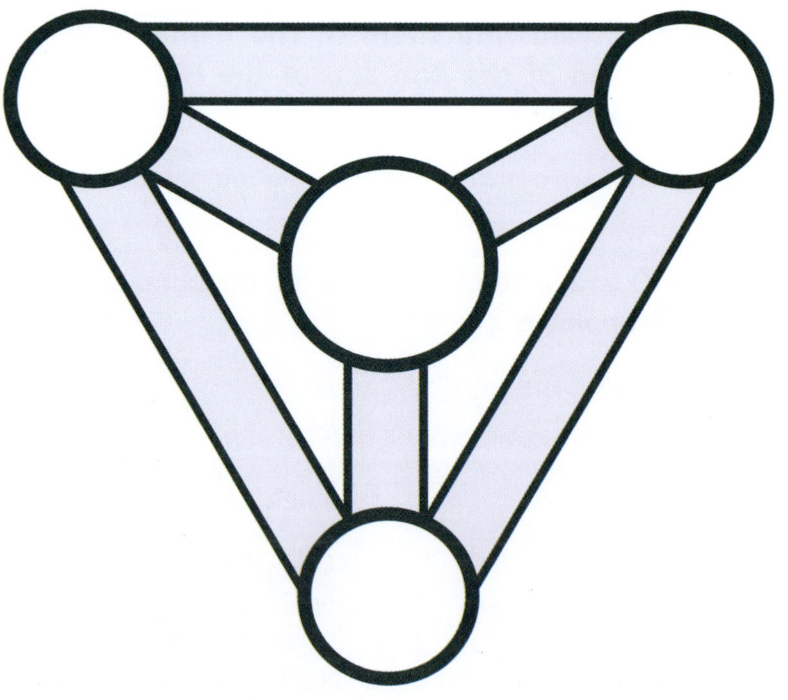

Does it look a little empty? It is! This drawing is referred to as the "Shield of the Trinity" and has been around since the twelfth century. It might be the closest we can come to having a picture of God. At the very least, this illustration helps us talk about God appropriately and is the closest we can come to a visual understanding of the Trinity.

Now's your chance to fill it in. **Go online and do an image search for "Shield of the Trinity"** (find one in English!) and **complete the blank drawing on the previous page**.

When you are through, you should be able to see certain phrases develop as you "read" the drawing, such as "The Father is God" and "The Son is not the Holy Spirit."

LOOKING FOR MORE?

Check out the Athanasian Creed for a very thorough explanation of the Holy Trinity. It can seem pretty long, but it is very helpful in teaching about our triune God!

Reflect

One of the things we talked about a lot in this lesson is how God has revealed Himself to us—that is, how God makes stuff known to us about who He is.

Pretend you live all alone on an island. You've never spoken to anyone in your life. What might you know about God?

Same island. What might you know about God's will for your life?

Turn in your Small Catechism to Question 105.

What are the three ways we can learn about God? These are the three ways God reveals Himself or makes Himself known. **Write these in the margin.** Be sure to use the language your catechism uses!

NOTES

Fill in the list below with things that you already know about the three persons of the Trinity. Take your time!

GOD THE FATHER	GOD THE SON	GOD THE HOLY SPIRIT
☐	☐	☐
☐	☐	☐
☐	☐	☐

Your Small Catechism has a ton of great stuff on the Trinity! Check out pages 128–32 for more information, questions, verses, and notes.

Scenario

The Roberts family from across the street invites your family over for a BBQ after church on Sunday. Mr. Roberts is talking with your parents about church, and he seems pretty curious (not aggressive—just curious). He says, "You guys go to Trinity Lutheran Church, right? That's one thing I've never quite been able to understand: the Trinity. How can God be one and three at the same time?" Your parents look at you (because you've read about this in confirmation).

What would you say to Mr. Roberts?

3.3 God Our Father

NOTES

As we continue to explore who God is (by reminding ourselves what He has done), we begin with the First Article of the Apostles' Creed.

This First Article (or paragraph or stanza) begins:

I believe in God, the Father Almighty . . .

The Apostles' Creed, like the Lord's Prayer, begins by calling God "Father." It's pretty amazing when you think about it. God is almighty (that is, all powerful), He's the Creator of all things, and He invites us to call Him "Father."

To some, that may be uncomfortable. By now, we know that our earthly fathers aren't always perfect—they're like us in that they make mistakes too. For some people, their earthly fathers have even hurt them or left them. When it comes to our heavenly Father, however, He's very different.

Open up your Small Catechism to the section on the First Article and read the answer to the question "What does this mean?"

Which parts of this answer stand out to you? **List at least three** in the space below:

This description from the Small Catechism is a summary of what we learn in Scripture. God provides for, takes care of, and protects us. Why does He do it? He's our heavenly Father. **He does it all "out of fatherly, divine goodness and mercy."**

NOTES

If you ever meet someone wondering why we refer to God this way, just keep in mind the three reasons that we see in Scripture. We call God "Father" because

- ☐ **Jesus does.** Jesus often refers to "the Father" during His ministry and also identifies Himself as "the Son." Reason number one that we call God "Father" is that we're listening to what Jesus said.
- ☐ **We're adopted.** Because of the work Jesus did for us on the cross, we've all been brought into the family of God. We're all His children through faith, so we call Him Father in response.
- ☐ **He provides.** As we mentioned above, in the same way we expect earthly fathers to provide for our needs, God never fails at providing what we need.

Ultimately, God revealed Himself in His Word as our Father, so we call Him "Father."

Read

Thinking about those three reasons why we call God "Father," take a look at the following passages below. On the right, you will see those three reasons we call God "Father." **Draw a line from each passage to the reason that it seems to connect with the most.** Multiple verses will match with certain reasons.

SCRIPTURE PASSAGE	REASONS WHY WE CALL GOD "FATHER"
Matthew 6:25–34	Jesus calls Him "Father."
John 3:16	
John 15:16	
	We are all His children.
John 20:17	
Galatians 3:26	
Ephesians 3:14	God provides for us.

Scenario

NOTES

Your friend Sabine has had a tough life. Her mom left her dad when she was six because he abused the family. Her father died just last year. Your family brought her to church, and it was Sabine's first time going. When you dropped her off at her house after lunch, you felt like everything had gone well. You catch her at school on Monday and ask her what she thought about church. She says, "It was really nice. Everyone was so kind. The only thing I didn't like was how much you guys called God 'Father.' Fathers are bad people. Why can't we just call God . . . well, God?"

From what you learned in this lesson, how would you respond to Sabine?

NOTES

3.4 The Creator

Are you near any flowers—real flowers? If you are, go take a look at them. If not, that's okay. Use your imagination.

Take some time to really examine the flower. Think about the way it feels, the way it smells. Take in the beauty of its colors and the complexity of its design.

As you observe this flower (whether with your hands or with your imagination), ask yourself this question: **What human could have made this?** We all know the answer. No one could. A fake flower is just not the same as a real one. Sure, they come pretty close, but nothing is like the real thing.

This goes for all of creation. Nothing is quite like the real thing and no human could create the incredible things we see in creation, no matter how hard he or she might try.

The second half of the First Article of the Apostles' Creed refers to God as

Maker of heaven and earth.

Need a refresher on what happened at creation? Head over to Genesis 1 and 2.

In those five words, we find one of the most foundational pieces for us to remember about God's identity: **He is the Creator**.

When we open up our Bibles to the very first verse, this is what we find:

> **In the beginning, God created the heavens and the earth.**
> **Genesis 1:1**

In that verse and the ones that follow, we see a powerful God, able to cause things to come into existence by simply saying the words "Let there be . . ." And we see a creative God who made incredible beauty and majesty, gigantic things and tiny things, simple organisms and complex systems.

It doesn't stop there. Look what we learn about who God is as He creates man:

Then the LORD God formed the man of dust from the ground and breathed into his nostrils the breath of life, and the man became a living creature. Genesis 2:7

Here we see the God who made us (mankind) in His own image. Not with words, but with His own hands. The God who gave us life by breathing His own breath into us. This is the God we call "Father."

When you confess the Apostles' Creed, you are saying that you believe God is the Creator of all things—that creation did not come from a big bang, or happen all by chance, or even just come from an intelligent designer, but that God created the world.

Understanding the world and our existence through this filter (that no one and nothing but God could do this creative work) sets up how we see ourselves and how we relate to God and the world around us.

For example, we begin to recognize these things about God:

- ☐ All of creation **belongs to Him**. It's not ours. He made all things and created humans to be stewards (or managers) of His creation. It's all a gift. Our families, the food on our table, the stuff that we have (even the stuff we sometimes waste)—it's all from God. He's entrusted it to us.
- ☐ God is **independent**. He doesn't need us. After all, He created the heavens and the earth without us! He's all powerful and all knowing without us.
- ☐ And yet . . . **He still created**. He didn't need creation; He wanted it. So He made the heavens and the earth.
- ☐ His **Word is powerful**. God created simply by speaking. The Bible doesn't say, "Then He gathered together all the materials and started building." No, it says that God spoke and things came into being. God said, "Let there be light," and there was light. Never underestimate the power of His Word!

Which one of these do you feel is most important for people to remember? Why?

NOTES

Same question for this set: Which one is most important ? Why?

This perspective also tells us a little more about creation itself:

- ☐ God **wanted** it. Because God is God, He doesn't need anything. When He created the world, He did so because He wanted it.
- ☐ God called His creation "**good**." Each day of creation, God looked at everything and "saw that it was good." On the final day, He called it "very good."
- ☐ God has a **relationship** with His creation. God may be independent, but His creation is very dependent. Without God's power and provision, creation would be toast! Creation needs its Creator.

Keep in mind that you are His creation too. That means that last section is about you too.

Ultimately, God may not need you but He does want you—He made you. When He looks at you (like when He looks at all things He creates), He calls you good. Finally, always remember that God has a relationship with you too. As His creation, you have a natural relationship with Him. We are utterly dependent on God for all that He provides, and He gladly provides for every need.

Read

MATTHEW 6:25–30

How does Jesus use the Father's work as Creator to tell you more about who God is?

What do these verses tell you about yourself as God's creation?

Scenarios

NOTES

Use the truths we learned about God and His creation on the opposite page to help respond to the following scenarios.

You're meeting a group of friends at the mall. This guy, Adam, is talking with your friends as you walk up. As you get closer, you overhear him saying, "I don't understand you guys. Why do you need 'God' in your lives anyway? My family has made it just fine without any of that nonsense. We provide for ourselves. We have plenty of money, and we don't waste our time with any of that mumbo jumbo religion stuff. There is no god. Your life will be better once you realize that." Your friends look at you for an answer.

What might you say?

Your friend Manuel seems pretty bummed out after practice. You sit down next to him and ask him what's going on. He says, "Nothing. I just feel pretty distant from God. Everyone else has families that all believe and stuff, but not me. I mean, I want to . . . you know . . . know God and stuff. I just feel like He doesn't want anything to do with me."

How would you respond to Manuel?

3.5 Who Is Jesus?

It's an important question: Who is Jesus? While we might be blessed to know many people who might have a good answer to this question, many of the people we will meet in our lives won't know how to begin to answer that question. It might even be a question that you haven't really wrestled with yet—and that's okay.

One of the first things that might have popped into your head when you read that question for the first time is, "Well . . . He's God." Exactly! As we learned in our lesson about the Trinity, one good answer to the question would be

Jesus is the Second Person of the Trinity.

He's God. But where do we learn this? How do we know Jesus is God? Many people say He was just a man or a good guy, so how do we know what is right and what is wrong? We could turn to our feelings—something like, "We just know!" Instead, let's turn to a place that never lets us down: God's Word.

What we learn about Jesus from John

Read John 1:1–17 and keep these verses open. This is a really important passage of Scripture (and it's not the only one, either!). One thing you'll notice is that John can be a little confusing. In this passage, John continually talks about "the Word." We might think that's a little weird. Why would John talk about the Bible so much, especially when the Bible hadn't been collected into all those books yet?

Exactly. John's talking about something else—or, more specifically, *someone* else.

We find our answer in John 1:17. That's the first time John gives a name to this person he's been calling "the Word." Throughout the whole passage, John has been talking about Jesus. Now that we know this is who John was referring to, we can make more sense of what John is telling us about Jesus.

Read John 1 again, but this time, every time you run into the phrase *the Word* or *the light*, insert the name Jesus instead. When you do this, it helps make more sense of what John is telling us about Jesus.

NOTES

Which phrases make more sense now that you've read it this way?

What we learn about Jesus from Genesis

In John 1, we learn that Jesus was present at creation. So why did He ultimately come to the world on that first Christmas? For that answer, we go to Genesis.

In Genesis 1 and 2, we learn how God created the world. On the sixth day of creation, God looked at everything He had made and described it as "very good." That didn't last long.

In Genesis 3, we learn about what we refer to as "the fall." This is when sin entered the world. God's perfect creation was no longer perfect and no longer how He designed it. But God made a promise! When talking with the serpent, God said:

> **I will put enmity between you and the woman, and between your offspring and her offspring. He shall bruise your head, and you shall bruise His heel. Genesis 3:15**

PRO TIP

Circle things in this section about Genesis that you think are most important!

The woman's offspring that God promised was Jesus. Eventually, Jesus would come into the world, born as a man (and therefore, the offspring of the woman). Jesus would ultimately "bruise" the serpent's head (defeat Satan) on the cross, where Satan would "strike His heel" (His death on the cross).

In other words, God promised from the very beginning that Jesus would come into the world to begin to restore all things to the way they were meant to be.

What we learn about Jesus from His name

Who is Jesus? Just look at His name. Do a quick internet search to find the meaning of both the name *Jesus* and the word *Christ*. Search something like "What does the name Jesus mean?" or "What does the word Christ mean?" **Fill in the blanks** when you find the answer.

The name Jesus means S________.

The word Christ means A ________ O________, or M ________.

What we learn about Jesus from His life

Who is Jesus? Look at His life. **Turn back to page 24 in this journal and look at #9. Write the phrases associated with each symbol below the symbol.**

Reflect

Look back at the last section about Jesus' life. We've always said that you can get to know who someone is by what they do. What do you think people can learn about who Jesus is by looking at what He did (and what He will do)?

Open up your Small Catechism to the section on the Second Article, and read the answer to the question "What does this mean?" (page 164).

Which parts of this answer stand out to you? **List at least three** in the space below.

Another fantastic answer to the question "Who is Jesus?" would be **Jesus is my Lord**. What does it mean for someone to have a lord?

Need some help brainstorming?

Think medieval! What would a lord do for their people? How would the people respond to their lord?

Scenario

You're walking with your parents in the city, and a man stops your family. He seems nice enough, and it turns out he's a student at a local Christian university. He says to your family, "This is a pretty Christian area, and for one of my classes, we're asking questions about Jesus." Your family isn't bothered, and they're open to answering his questions. The man then says, "Jesus is very important for Christians—obviously. But when you come to think of it, then why wasn't Jesus a part of the picture until thousands of years after creation?"

Keeping in mind what you learned about Jesus from John 1 and Genesis, how would you contribute to the conversation?

NOTES

3.6 True God, True Man

Is Jesus God or man?

We know that Jesus is God. We saw this in John 1 and know many other places in Scripture attest to this as well. He's the Second Person of the Trinity. We also know He was born of Mary. He walked this earth as a man, was crucified, died, and was buried.

So is Jesus God or man? The answer is yes. Is Jesus Creator or creation? Well, yes.

Jesus is both fully God and fully man. That's what we learn when we turn to Scripture. If you had to give it a percentage, we would say:

Jesus is 100 percent man and 100 percent God.

Did you know the word *incarnation* literally means "in the flesh"? The Spanish word for meat comes from the same Latin word, *carnem*.

Jesus is both God and man. This began at Christ's incarnation (that is, when Jesus was conceived of the Holy Spirit by the Virgin Mary) and continues forever. Prior to the incarnation, Jesus still existed. We learned this in John 1. He was, is, and always will be God. Once He took on flesh, however, He has not just one nature but two.

We refer to this as the **two natures of Christ**. We would say that God (that is, the Holy Trinity) has one nature: He's God. But we also recognize that He reveals Himself as three persons: Father, Son, and Holy Spirit. The Second Person of the Trinity, Jesus, is unique in that He is one person with two natures (God and man).

Read

We've already seen what John 1 has to say about Jesus being God. We're also confident that Jesus was a man who walked this earth. **Look up these other Scripture verses** that tell us Jesus is also God and **fill in the blanks**.

John 20:28 Thomas answered Him, "My ______ and my ______!"

Romans 9:5 From their race, according to the flesh, is the ______, who is ______ over all, blessed forever.

1 John 5:20 And we know that the Son of God has come and has given us understanding, so that we may know Him who is true; and we are in Him who is true, in His Son ______ ______. He is the true ______ and eternal life.

Colossians 2:9 For in Him the ______ fullness of ______ dwells bodily.

Jesus Has Become Our Brother

As a result of the incarnation, the Son of God, the Creator of the universe, became man, sharing our humanity in all things except sin. In this way, Jesus has become our Brother. He knows what it is to be human—He is one. You might be asking yourself, why is this important?

Open your Small Catechism to Questions 159 and 160, and complete the chart below.

WHY IS IT IMPORTANT THAT JESUS IS FULLY MAN?	WHY IS IT IMPORTANT THAT JESUS IS FULLY GOD?

NOTES

Scenarios

Your cousin Bart stopped going to church after he got confirmed. Curious, you ask him, “So, Bart, you went through that whole confirmation process, but now you don’t even go to church—what gives?” Bart shrugs, “I dunno. I just watched some YouTube videos about Jesus, and I really think He’s nothing more than a good dude. I mean, I like what He says and all—and it’s nice to hear you’re forgiven and loved—but He was just a man. I don’t believe all that God stuff about Him.”

What things could you remind Bart about that might help him rethink what he said about Jesus?

At lunch, your friend Penny taps you on the shoulder. She says, “Hey, Brian is asking questions that I don’t know how to answer.” You come to find out Brian is asking the group how it is possible that one person could die for the sins of the whole world. In Brian’s words, “No one dude’s life could take away the sin for millions. It’s just doesn’t make any sense.”

With Jesus being both fully man and fully God, how do you respond to Brian?

3.7 Prophet, Priest, King

NOTES

When you hear the word *Messiah*, what comes to mind?

In the season of Advent (the time that leads up to Christmas), the Church naturally talks a whole lot about how God's people would have been looking forward to the coming of the Messiah. During that season, we revisit many places in the Old Testament where we can see that the Messiah they were expecting was Jesus.

What's interesting as we look at the Old Testament, however, is that God's people weren't necessarily looking forward to just one Messiah but many. Think about the number of people in the time of the Old Testament who were "anointed." (Saul and David come to mind.) Each one of them would have been seen as someone who could finally bring the deliverance that God had promised to His people.

To be anointed meant that you were chosen, that the Lord's Spirit would be upon you, and it was often accompanied by an actual anointing with oil. When we look at the Old Testament, we see that there were primarily three types of people God would choose as messiahs (or "anointed ones"): **prophets**, **priests**, and **kings**.

What's important to remember is the role that each one would play:

- ☐ A **prophet** would be chosen to proclaim God's Word.
- ☐ A **priest** would be chosen to atone for the sins of the people and intercede with God on behalf of them.
- ☐ A **king** would be chosen to rule over the people.

When you think about messiahs from this perspective, you can see many people in the Old Testament God chose to fulfill these roles over time.

When we turn to the New Testament, only one person bears that title. And here's what we learn about Him:

Jesus isn't just a messiah, He's *the* Messiah.

NOTES

Jesus isn't just another one in a line of many—Jesus is *the* Messiah because He fulfills all three roles. Jesus is the only person in the history of God's people to hold all three offices simultaneously. As a **prophet**, Jesus guides us as He proclaims His Word. As a **priest**, He forgives our sins and intercedes with the Father on our behalf. As a **king**, He rules over our lives.

Read

Write key phrases that helped you identify the office here:

Look up the verses below. Each one will match with one of the three offices that Jesus holds. **Draw a line connecting the verse to the office it relates to**, and **out to the side, write down the key phrases** from that verse that help you see how Jesus is the fulfillment of that office.

COLOSSIANS 1:17–18	Prophet
MATTHEW 17:5	Priest
HEBREWS 7:26–27	King

Scenario

You're hanging out with your friend Hannah at the park after a soccer game. Hannah and her family are Jewish. She knows you are a Christian and that you believe something about Jesus being the Messiah that was promised. She asks you, "Why do you think Jesus is the Messiah? As I read through our Scripture, there are many people who were anointed to do the Lord's work. What is different about Jesus than all the other messiahs?"

How might you respond to Hannah?

3.8 Two States: Humiliation and Exaltation

We've spent a lot of time talking about who Jesus is and what He has done, but it's been a while since we've spent time with the words of the Second Article of the Apostles' Creed. Before we close this section on Jesus, let's revisit those words:

> [I believe] in Jesus Christ, His only Son, our Lord, who was conceived by the Holy Spirit, born of the Virgin Mary, suffered under Pontius Pilate, was crucified, died and was buried. He descended into hell. The third day He rose again from the dead. He ascended into heaven and sits at the right hand of God, the Father Almighty. From thence He will come to judge the living and the dead.

As a man, Jesus did not always fully use His divine powers and majesty that were communicated to His human nature. In other words, even though He was God, He didn't always exercise His divinity. We see this beginning with the lowly manner of His incarnation and continuing in the manner of His birth and life, and ultimately with His death and burial. We call this His **state of humiliation**.

At the same time, there were times when Jesus did exercise His divinity. At certain points, He made His divine power and majesty visible during His early life with miracles and especially at the transfiguration (see Matthew 17:1–13). We also see Jesus fully exercise His power and divinity constantly and completely in His victorious descent into hell, His resurrection from the dead, His ascension into heaven, His present reign at the right hand of God, and His future return for judgment. We call this His **state of exaltation**.

NOTES

To help you visualize these two states, complete the following charts.

JESUS' STATE OF HUMILIATION

(Jesus humbled Himself by not exercising His divinity.)

__________ by the Holy Spirit

__________ of the Virgin Mary

__________ under Pontius Pilate

was __________ , died and was buried

Read

PHILIPPIANS 2:5–8

Which of the two states (humiliation or exaltation) connects to these verses? What phrases help you to see this?

Philippians 2:1–11 is an incredibly important piece of Scripture. If you've ever wanted to commit Scripture to memory, this is a good passage to start with!

PHILIPPIANS 2:9–11

Which of the two states connects to these verses? What phrases help you to see this?

JESUS' STATE OF EXALTATION

(Jesus exalted Himself by exercising His divinity fully.)

__________ at the right hand of God

He __________ into heaven

The third day He __________ again from the dead

He __________ into hell

The "descended into hell" part of the Creed tends to throw people off. We're reminded that this part of the Creed is a part of His exaltation even though it uses the word *descended*, because Jesus is proclaiming His victory in hell. **Read 1 Peter 3:18–20** as a reference (verse 19 is the key verse).

Scenarios

You and your friend Bobby are playing video games after church one day. Bobby doesn't really go to church, so the whole thing was a little new to him. You're talking with him about it, and he mentions the Creed. He notices, "That whole part about saying hell in church was a little strange. I mean, I didn't even think people still believed in hell. What was that all about?"

You've got an opportunity to talk about Jesus' victory here (in His exaltation). How do you respond to Bobby?

It's Thanksgiving time. Cousin Bart is back in the picture. What you said about Jesus being fully God really stuck with him. Now he can't wrap his head around the fact that Jesus (being God) would ever become man. He says, "You made such good points last time, especially when you showed me all those places in Scripture where it talks about Jesus being God too. Now I'm starting to think He was never really a man. I mean, why would God—an infinite being—want to become a finite man?"

Thinking about what you read in Philippians 2, how do you respond to Bart in a way that would help him understand why Jesus would become man?

3.9 The Holy Spirit Is a Life-Giver

NOTES

Of the three persons of the Trinity, the Holy Spirit is easily the most difficult to grasp. He has no physical presence like Jesus did and no earthly parallel like God the Father. But the Holy Spirit is constantly at work in the hearts of those who believe in Jesus Christ.

In John 11, Jesus raises Lazarus from the dead. **Go ahead and look it up.** (It's a quick read.) By the time Jesus gets to him, Lazarus has been dead for four days. Even so, Jesus has the stone moved away from Lazarus's tomb and calls to him, "Lazarus, come out." And he did. This dead man, at Jesus' call, came back to life.

In response to the question "What does this mean?" for Part 1 of the Third Article, the Small Catechism reads:

> I believe that I cannot by my own reason or strength believe in Jesus Christ, my Lord, or come to Him; but the Holy Spirit has called me by the Gospel, enlightened me with His gifts, sanctified and kept me in the true faith.

On our own, we are spiritually dead, like Lazarus was physically dead. However, notice in the meaning of the Third Article above, we see that the Holy Spirit "has called me by the Gospel."

Just like Jesus' call to Lazarus raised him from the dead, the Holy Spirit's call to us by the Gospel raises us from spiritual death and into life. This is why the Nicene Creed says, "I believe in the Holy Spirit, the Lord and giver of life." The Holy Spirit brings us to Jesus by bringing the promise of the Gospel to us, which gives us faith in Jesus through that Gospel. In other words, **the Holy Spirit is a life-giver**.

NOTES

Reflect

Lazarus likely had a new perspective on life after being raised from the dead. What do you think was different for him?

The Holy Spirit calls you to new life too—a life of following Jesus as Lord. What is the danger of ignoring the Holy Spirit's call in your life?

Read

The Holy Spirit is a giver. There's no doubt about it. **Look up the following passages and write in the space provided** what these verses say the Holy Spirit does or gives to us as believers who have heard the Gospel.

JOHN 14:26

JOHN 16:13

ROMANS 8:16

ROMANS 8:26

Ephesians 2:1 reminds us, "You were dead in your trespasses and sins" before the Holy Spirit brought you new life by faith. Romans 6:23 also reminds us of this when it says, "For the wages of sin is death." The Bible also has many reminders of what the Spirit has done in your life; He has called you by the Gospel to give you faith, which leads to eternal life.

Look up the following verses in your personal Bible and highlight them so that you can be reminded of this promise every time you see them.

- ☐ **2 Thessalonians 2:14** To this He called you through our gospel, so that you may obtain the glory of our Lord Jesus Christ.
- ☐ **Romans 1:16** For I am not ashamed of the gospel, for it is the power of God for salvation to everyone who believes, to the Jew first and also to the Greek.
- ☐ **Romans 10:17** So faith comes from hearing, and hearing through the word of Christ.
- ☐ **Ephesians 1:13** In Him you also, when you heard the word of truth, the gospel of your salvation, and believed in Him, were sealed with the promised Holy Spirit.

Reflect

The Holy Spirit is called a guide, teacher, faith-giver, and intercessor for us. He gives us courage to turn away from sin, confidence in Jesus' promises, and hope in really hard situations. Identify one area of your life where you've seen the Holy Spirit at work and one where you'd like to pray for strengthening in that area.

An area where I've seen the Holy Spirit work:

An area where I'd like to pray for strengthening:

NOTES

3.10 And a Gift-Giver and a Fruit-Producer

The Holy Spirit is a gift-giver.

Remember when you were little and Christmas or your birthday was coming? What kind of gifts did you want? Probably toys, right? Whatever toy was the next big thing, that was usually the one you'd ask for. As you get older, you'll start to notice your wish list starts to change. Instead of just asking for things that are fun, you might find yourself asking for gifts that might be a little more useful: a cell phone, a computer, a car. As we get older, we seem to want things that help us do what we want to do (or need to do) better.

The Holy Spirit is a gift-giver. He doesn't give us Easy-Bake Ovens, or fishing poles, or iPads. He gives us spiritual gifts.

> **Having gifts that differ according to the grace given to us, let us use them: if prophecy, in proportion to our faith; if service, in our serving; the one who teaches, in his teaching; the one who exhorts, in his exhortation; the one who contributes, in generosity; the one who leads, with zeal; the one who does acts of mercy, with cheerfulness. Romans 12:6–8**

Because God has made each of us unique, He has unique work in mind for each of us to do, and He gives each of us a set of gifts in order to accomplish that job. The gifts of the Holy Spirit all work together, in each of us, to help the Church (God's people) fulfill its purpose: sharing the Gospel with the world.

The Holy Spirit is a fruit-producer.

How can you tell if a tree is an apple tree? By apples growing on it. How can you tell if someone is living a life filled by the Spirit? By the spiritual fruit they produce.

But the fruit of the Spirit is love, joy, peace, patience, kindness, goodness, faithfulness, gentleness, self-control; against such things there is no law. And those who belong to Christ Jesus have crucified the flesh with its passions and desires. If we live by the Spirit, let us also keep in step with the Spirit. Galatians 5:22–25

When Paul writes his letter to the Galatians, he includes this list of nine fruits that the Holy Spirit produces in the life of a believer in Jesus. In the case of spiritual *gifts*, we each have a unique combination given to us by the Holy Spirit. But in the case of spiritual *fruit*, God wants to produce all of them in each of us. A mark of spiritual maturity is how the fruit of the Spirit is shown in our lives.

Reflect

When you read the list of spiritual gifts in Romans 12, which ones sound most like you? Why?

When you look at the list of the fruit of the Spirit in Galatians 5, which ones come easiest for you? Which are more difficult? Why?

NOTES

NOTES

Find a parent or trusted adult (who knows you well) and follow the directions below.

Say, "We're talking about how God gives each of us unique spiritual gifts. What unique gifts do you see in me?" Write his or her response below.

Share with that same adult the fruit of the Spirit from Galatians 5:22–25. Then say, "Which ones do you see most in me?" Write his or her responses here.

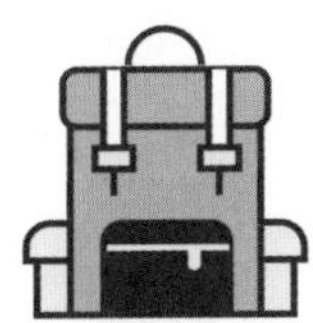

3.11 And Does a Lot More

The Third Article of the Apostles' Creed seems to cover a lot of ground. As we learned at the start of this unit, the Apostles' Creed is basically a summary of what we know from the Bible. It sums up for us what God has done and how God has made Himself known. The First Article talks about God the Father, the Second Article about God the Son, and the Third Article covers the Holy Spirit . . . and the Church, saints, forgiveness, resurrection, and eternal life.

Was the Third Article just a catch-all? A place to add all the little bits and pieces about what we believe before they finished writing the Creed? Not at all! What we find when we take a look at God's Word is that the Third Article seems to cover a lot of ground because the Holy Spirit also covers a lot of ground. He does a lot more than we often think about.

Let's take a look at some of these things listed in the Third Article:

I believe in . . . the holy Christian church, the communion of saints . . .

- ☐ **Read Ephesians 2:19–22.** This part of the Creed is tricky because it uses the words *church* and *communion* in different ways than we normally use them.
- ☐ Usually when people say "church," they're talking about a building, like, "I'm going to church." The Bible uses that word in an entirely different way. When it uses the word *church*, it's referring to people. Everyone who shares faith in Jesus as Lord and Savior is a member of the holy Christian church.
- ☐ Similarly, when we hear the word *communion*, we usually think of Christ's body and blood during a worship service. In the Creed, however, *communion* means something more like "to be joined in fellowship" or "a deep relationship."

NOTES

- On a large scale, this means that when we say we believe in the holy Christian church and the communion of saints, we are really saying that we believe **we are joined together, by faith, with all those who believe in Jesus**. That's a big church!
- On a smaller scale, we're also saying that we believe being a part of a local congregation is important. Worshiping regularly with other Christians and being connected with other believers studying God's Word are ways the Holy Spirit does His work of keeping us in the true faith.

I believe in the . . . forgiveness of sins . . .

- **Read 1 John 1:9.** It's pretty self-explanatory, but it's worth repeating: we believe that **because of Jesus' death and resurrection, God will not hold our sins against us**. Our sins are forgiven!

I believe in . . . the resurrection of the body, and the life everlasting.

- **Read Job 19:25–27.** Scripture is very clear about the resurrection of the dead. When we die, our body and spirit are separated. That's why it's okay to call death "bad" and why death was not a part of God's original design. That's also why God did something about it. Jesus died and rose again so that you and I would receive the gift of faith that leads to eternal life. **Jesus' promise for us as believers is that, in Him, we will be raised to eternal life.** When Jesus returns, body and spirit will be reunited once and for all, and we will live the life God originally intended for His creation.

Remember to request the Spirit.

How do all these things that close out the Creed connect with the Holy Spirit? They all connect to faith, which is a gift of the Holy Spirit, and that gift **leads to life**. Through faith, the Holy Spirit works within the **Church** (God's people) to gather us into **communion** (that is, fellowship) with one another to nurture and strengthen our faith through the Word of God. That Word also speaks to us the precious words of the Gospel that offer us **forgiveness**. In faith, we hear those words as God sanctifies and renews us. That Word is also God's means to deliver faith, which leads to **eternal life** that will follow the coming **resurrection** of all who have died in the faith.

The Holy Spirit is up to a lot in our lives. Never underestimate what He is doing.

NOTES

Reflect

How has your connection to a Christian community brought you closer to God's Word (which gives life)?

Make a list in the margin of people that the Holy Spirit has used in your life to teach you about the importance of faith. **In the space below, write a prayer of thanks** to God for using these people and for their faithfulness.

Who is one person you could ask the Holy Spirit to help you share more about your faith with? **Pray for that person now.**

NOTES

Unit 3 Reflection

In the past eleven lessons, you've had the opportunity to explore the identity of our amazing God. For this final reflection, **fill in the remaining space on this page with what you are taking away from this unit.** Think back on all that you've explored. Pretend this page is a study guide for a big test that your teacher allows you to take with you into a test. Write down everything that comes to mind anywhere that you'd like! These prompts can help get you started:

Creator or creation?

Why do we call God "Father"?

What does the Father do?

What did Jesus do?

What does the Spirit do?

What's the Apostles' Creed?

Write a prayer to God now that you've explored who He is.

You have completed Unit 3.

Finish your Unit Check-In.

Unit 4

How Do I Live My Life?

NOTES

It might be a little intimidating to think about standing before God's throne, especially now that we know who He is.

He's the one who created all things by simply speaking, the one who overcame death and the grave for our sakes, the one who has the power to bring life from death, the one who still speaks through His Word, and the one who is simply far beyond what any of our minds could ever fully comprehend.

Standing before His throne, you're reminded of His purpose for your life: to love Him and love your neighbor. You're reminded that He created you, that He sent His Son to die for you so that you would live, and that He continues to pour out His gifts into your life through His Spirit.

But you're also reminded that He invites you to stand there before His throne. And that brings up another pretty important question:

> **God, as Your redeemed child, how do I live my life in such a way that I daily receive Your gifts and commend my life to Your care?**

It's easy to lose sight of who God is and what He wants for your life. It's easy to forget how vital it is that we commend our lives to His care, instead of relying solely on ourselves. God knows this about us, so He gave us something that would help us find the answer to the question "How do I live my life?" **He gave us the Lord's Prayer.**

In the words Jesus gives to us in His model prayer, we discover what it truly means to desire God's gifts and entrust our lives to His care. As we step before His throne, His words give us both perspective and direction for our daily lives.

Before you begin this unit, write the phrase "I will live" above the title of every lesson as a reminder that when you pray the Lord's Prayer, each petition is reminding you how to live your life in such a way that you daily receive His gifts and commend your life to Him.

NOTES

4.1 Talking to God

Whom do you have in your life that you feel like you can talk to about anything? Maybe it's a parent, a close friend, a trusted adult, or a mentor. Having someone like that in your life gives you a sense of security and safety because you can be honest and open about whatever is on your mind without fear of judgment or shame. It helps you to feel seen, heard, and understood.

Even if you can't think of someone off the top of your head who matches the description above, God is always willing to listen. That's why God gave us this gift we call prayer. Through our prayers, we bring to God our needs, our hopes, our hurts, our joys, and anything and everything else that comes our way.

But what exactly is prayer? Let's keep it simple:

Prayer is talking to God in words and thoughts.

Ever read the part of the Gospels where Jesus teaches His disciples the Lord's Prayer? Read it for yourself in Luke 11:1–4 or Matthew 6:9–13.

That's right! It's as easy as talking. What would you say to the One who made you, redeemed you, and sustains your everyday life? What would you say to the One who has power over all creation? Would you thank Him? ask Him for something? fill Him in on how things are going? seek His advice and wisdom?

Prayer is both one of the easiest and hardest habits for a Christian. It's easy in the sense that it doesn't require any special talents or abilities. It's hard because it takes time, focus, and practice. Either way we look at it, prayer is certainly one of the most important habits for a Christian.

While prayer might seem a little intimidating for some, remember that prayer doesn't require any special training—you don't have to be a pastor to be able to pray. You just need to be willing to talk! It's that simple.

Read

MATTHEW 6:5–8

How might these verses give you confidence to pray more often?

What do you think is the most important thing someone should remember about prayer? Why?

Open up your Small Catechism and explore pages 231–36 on prayer.

Make notes in your catechism for what stands out to you. Some great things to do would be to **star (*), underline, highlight, or circle anything you find particularly meaningful**.

Pray

For every lesson in this unit, you'll be asked to write a prayer at the conclusion. You will also have some space in the margin to write prayer requests. Go ahead and **write your prayer requests** there now.

Take a few minutes to reflect upon what it means to talk with God, as well as on your prayer requests. Set a timer, clear your head, and just think about those things. Use the space below to talk with God *now*. Write the prayer that comes to mind. Fill every line! God wants to hear from you. Talk to Him.

Dear God,

. . . In the name of Jesus. Amen.

NOTES

Getting Started with Prayer

There's a lot of freedom when it comes to prayer. These pages are meant to help you get started with some ways to pray! Think of these two pages as a lot of good advice when you get stuck wondering what to pray.

THE ACTS PRAYER

To pray this style of prayer, think of **ACTS**:

ADORATION. Praise God for who He is.
Lord, You are wise, loving, kind, strong, pure . . .

CONFESSION. Confess your sins and ask for forgiveness.
Lord, forgive me for . . .

THANKSGIVING. Thank God for what He's done.
Thank You, Lord, for my home, church, family . . .

SUPPLICATION. Ask God to help you and others.
Give me strength to believe and help my mom get better . . .

MARTIN LUTHER'S "SIMPLE WAY TO PRAY"

Luther created this style of prayer that he could use with the words of the Ten Commandments, the Lord's Prayer, the Creed, or any passage from the Bible. He saw it as a way to let the Holy Spirit guide his thoughts as he prayed through God's Word:

INSTRUCTION. Read the text slowly. What words jump out to you? trouble you? encourage or comfort you? What is it teaching you?

THANKSGIVING. What do you have to be thankful for in the text?

CONFESSION. What can you confess?

PRAY. Now pray using the above three things to guide your prayer. Just start talking to God!

CIRCLE-OUT PRAYER

For this style of prayer, start with yourself and then gradually pray for groups greater than yourself:

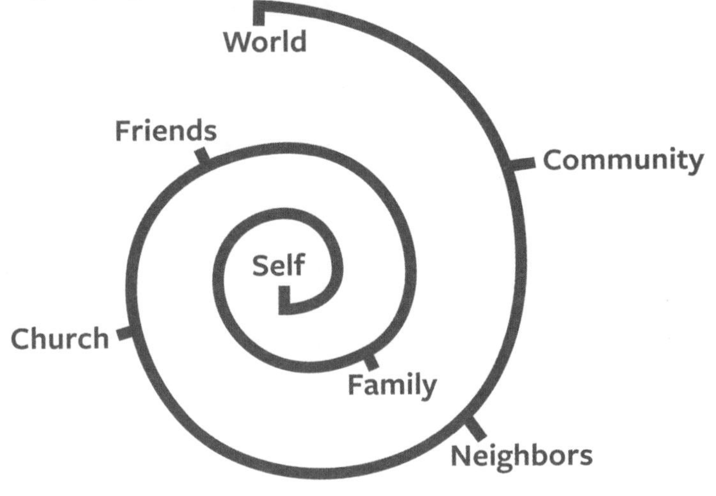

TYPES OF PRAYERS

SPONTANEOUS PRAYERS. These are prayers when you just say what comes to your mind and your heart. Whatever words come to you are the words you pray.

PRAYERS FROM THE BIBLE. The Bible is full of prayers! When you don't have words, the Bible has them for you. Check out the Book of Psalms specifically! Lots of great prayers can be found in there.

WRITTEN PRAYERS. Sometimes, you know you'll be asked to pray for something, and you might find it easier to write it out ahead of time. That's great! Written prayers are still prayers. If you ever find yourself getting nervous about praying, try writing it down.

PRAYERS FROM MEMORY. There are some pretty great prayers out there that have already been written. There's no shame in saying a prayer that you've already memorized! The important thing is to pray them from the heart. We don't want to be robots when we pray. We want to mean what we say!

NOTES

Remember, you can talk to God anywhere at anytime! You can pray with your eyes open or closed, you can talk out loud or in your head. The important thing is that you're talking with God.

WHEN DO I PRAY?

Unlike other religions, we don't have specific times we are expected to pray. However, there are some good opportunities to pray each day. For instance, in the morning when you get up and at night when you go to sleep are great times to give thanks to God. Meal times are another great opportunity!

DAILY PRAYERS

Speaking of prayers from memory, at the front of your Small Catechism, you will find a section called "Daily Prayers." Here you'll find Martin Luther's Morning and Evening Prayers, along with ways to pray before and after a meal. Check it out!

PRACTICE, PRACTICE, PRACTICE

No one starts out just knowing how to pray. It takes practice! Be intentional about finding opportunities to pray each day. Make it a habit to write a prayer down each week. Volunteer every once and a while to say a prayer for your family or small group. We all start somewhere! You can do it.

LOOK IT UP

Sometimes the words just aren't coming to us. Sometimes we can't even find words in places we'd usually look, like our Bible. Don't be afraid to do a quick search, such as "prayers for anxiety," if you just can't seem to find the words to say to God. Some devotionals or prayer books have lists like this. You never know what you might find!

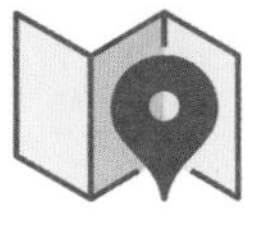

4.2 As a Family, Under the Father

NOTES

Our Father.

With these two words, Jesus begins His model prayer. For some of us, the word *father* is a pretty formal title for your dad. What's interesting when Jesus teaches this prayer, however, is that it's actually a pretty unique word. Here, Jesus is using the Aramaic word *abba*, which means something along the lines of *daddy* or *papa*. It's not a formal title at all. Quite the opposite: it's endearing. It's intimate. It's respectful. It's something you would only call someone you were close with.

So as Jesus begins this model prayer, He's saying,

It's okay to call God *Papa*.

Think about how this changes our approach to God. Yes, He's still God. He's still the Creator of the universe, bigger and greater than anything we could imagine; but He has also asked us to call Him Papa. Once again, God is reaffirming that you are His child. As the Small Catechism puts it:

> With these words God tenderly invites us to believe that
> He is our true Father and that we are His true children,
> so that with all boldness and confidence we may ask
> Him as dear children ask their dear father.

These two words are also reminders that we aren't alone. Jesus doesn't begin His model prayer, "My Father," He says, "Our Father." You'll notice this sort of communal language throughout the Lord's Prayer. It's a reminder that we are a part of a much bigger family and that we're all in this together.

Even in these first two words, we learn a little about how we ought to live our lives. We live together as the family of God, under the direction of our Papa.

NOTES

Read

Open your Small Catechism to Questions 244 and 245, and pay special attention to the Bible verses.

What are some of the responsibilities God has toward you as Father, according to these verses?

As His child, you are able to approach Him with confidence when you need help. Which verse from this section assures you of that promise?

Reflect

What makes a great dad? What does he do for his children?

Why would the almighty God invite us to call Him something as ordinary as Father?

What sort of relationship would a child have with their father if they never talked to their father?

Pray

Take a few minutes to reflect upon what it means that God is your Father. Consider your prayer requests. Focus and just think about those things. **Now use the space below to talk with God. Write the prayer that comes to mind.** Just talk to your Papa.

NOTES

Heavenly Father, Abba,

. . . In the name of Jesus. Amen.

NOTES

4.3 Keeping God's Name Holy

Hallowed be Thy name.

God is serious about His name and how we use it. Look back at your lesson on the Second Commandment. When we pray the First Petition of the Lord's Prayer, "Hallowed be Thy name," we're asking God to help us keep this commandment as well.

Hallowed is a word that means something along the lines of holy, sacred, or reverend. When we pray "Hallowed be Thy name," we're declaring to God that His name is like His character: holy—pure, set apart, perfect, totally *other* when compared to anything else in all of creation. Are you getting the picture?

Now, telling God that His name is holy is not news to Him. Rather, as we pray "Hallowed be Thy name," it's as if we're saying, "Your name is holy; I recognize that. Now, help me to live a life that reflects that truth."

In other words, **we're not so much asking that God's name be made holy, but rather that He would help us to keep His name holy.**

And how is God's name kept holy? That's the question Martin Luther asked when he was putting together the Small Catechism.

Open your Small Catechism up to the section on the First Petition of the Lord's Prayer, and read the answer to that question.

What stands out to you about what you read in your Small Catechism?

Here are two important phrases that stand out:

When the Word of God is taught in its truth and purity . . .

We, as the children of God, also lead holy lives according to it.

NOTES

When we pray this part of the Lord's Prayer, we are asking that God would help us to keep His name holy by helping us to **speak truthfully about God's Word and also live according to it**.

As Christians, God expects us to be His representatives. When we uphold His truth and live according to it, His name is kept holy. When we don't, His name is profaned. As we pray these words together, we're asking that God would direct the way we live our lives in such a way that **His name is kept holy by all that we think, all that we say, and all that we do**.

Reflect

What makes God holy? What can you say about God that you can't say about anyone or anything else?

How can a person in today's world keep God's name holy? When is it most difficult to live according to God's Word or preserve His truth?

Pray

Reflect on what it means to keep God's name holy, and consider your prayer requests. **Now use the space below to talk with God. Write the prayer that comes to mind.** Talk to the One who is set apart, pure, and perfect.

Most Holy God,

. . . In the name of Jesus. Amen.

NOTES

4.4 Desiring His Kingdom

Thy kingdom come.

Jesus has a lot to say about the kingdom of God during His earthly ministry. In fact, the Gospels mention the word *kingdom* over 120 times. It's clear that Jesus wants us to know about the kingdom.

But what exactly is the kingdom of God? My guess is that most people think back to medieval times when they hear the word *kingdom*. You have your castle, you have your boundaries, you have your citizens, and, of course, you have your king. When we hear Jesus talk in the Gospels, however, it's clear that He defines this word *kingdom* differently. When He talks about the kingdom of God, He's talking about **God's kingly rule**. He's talking about God's reign, His action, His lordship, and His sovereign governance.

In other words, wherever God is King, there you will find the kingdom.

God's kingdom is not a realm or a people, nor is it defined by geographical boundaries. Now, the kingdom does create a realm and it does create a people, but the kingdom of God is not synonymous with its realm or its people. The kingdom of God is defined by where and when (or within whom) God is king.

So where is this kingdom? We like to think of God's kingdom in three main ways. God's kingdom is

- ☐ **Everywhere**—As Creator of the entire universe, God is ruler over all—there's really no way around it. We think of this as God's ***kingdom of power***.
- ☐ **Where God's Word is spread or heard**—The Word of God is living and active, and it moves throughout Christ's Church, all believers (remember Lesson 3.11!). Wherever it is seen and heard, people come under the reign and rule of God. We refer to this as God's ***kingdom of grace***.
- ☐ **Still coming with Jesus**—There is an incredible Day still yet to come when Jesus will return and we will know the kingdom in a very full and perfect way. There will be no more

sorrow, sin, or death, and God's reign and rule will be very evident. We refer to this as God's ***kingdom of glory***.

Every time we pray this petition of the Lord's Prayer, it's a reminder that it is our most sincere desire for God's reign and rule to come into our world and our lives. After all, we couldn't ask for a better King! He gave everything for His kingdom so that we could live eternally with Him. Because of that, we pray for His kingdom to come.

Look up Question 257 in your Small Catechism.

Make notes about what stands out most to you as you are reading. Feel free to mark it up!

Reflect

Who is someone with whom you could share God's Word and, in so doing, welcome into God's kingdom of grace?

What do you think will be the best part when Jesus comes back in glory?

Pray

Reflect on God's kingdom and what it means that God is ruler over all. Add your prayer requests. Focus and just think about those things. **Now use the space below to talk with God.**

Bringer of the Kingdom,

. . . In the name of Jesus. Amen.

NOTES

4.5 Pursuing His Will

Thy will be done.

> **Because Satan, the world, and our sinful flesh are the three things that oppose God's will, we refer to them as the "unholy trinity."**

The difference between "Thy will be done" and "my will be done" doesn't look like much when you read it on paper. It's just a one-word difference. The difference in our hearts, however, is enormous. We tend to live our lives in a "my will be done" mindset because of our sinful nature. We say to ourselves, "I'll do what I want to do! God, You stay over there and let me live life my way." That's why this petition of the Lord's Prayer is a total game changer.

Praying "Thy will be done" is saying to God, "I trust in You. I know Your ways are perfect and mine are not. You know what is best. Accomplish Your will in me and through me, God. Show me Your will, and I will pursue it."

And what is God's will? We read in Question 261:

God's will is that all people come to know Him as their Father and live under the reign and rule of His Son.

When we pray this petition of the Lord's Prayer, we are asking that God, in keeping with His will, would never allow Satan, the world, and our sinful flesh to take God's name and faith from us.

But how can we tell what God's will is for our lives? Here are four questions to ask yourself when trying to determine God's will in a certain situation:

> **Next time you find yourself facing a big decision, return to these questions!**

- ☐ **What does the Bible have to say about it?** If what you're considering is against what the Bible says, it's not God's will—it's yours. A good rule of thumb is to ask yourself, "Does this help me to love God or love my neighbor?" If the answer is yes to both, there's a good chance it lines up with God's will.
- ☐ **What's the wisdom of a mature Christian whom I trust?** God places people in our lives for a reason. If you're struggling with a decision, ask a trusted adult, a mentor, or a parent. God uses people like this to help us consider His will. Ask them!

- ☐ **What is the Spirit telling me through the circumstances?** Weigh the options. Ask yourself, "Does this make sense for all the circumstance in my life right now? What will be the challenges? What will be the benefits?" You'll find that God often works things out for us in advance through the circumstances leading up to a big decision.
- ☐ **Have I prayed over it?** It's important that prayer is a part of it. Spend plenty of time praying—a few days, if not longer! It's also important that prayer is not the only step you take. If all we do is pray, we might be tempted to go back to "my will" (doing nothing despite prayer) rather than "Thy will" (taking action, guided by the Holy Spirit).

Jesus prays this phrase twice during His earthly ministry. Once is when He teaches the disciples His model prayer. The second is when He is preparing His heart for His death while praying to the Father in the Garden of Gethsemane. He says, "Father, not My will but Yours be done." He could have called down legions of angels to come and rescue Him from that moment, but He didn't. **Look up some images of Jesus praying in the garden.**

Is this how you've pictured Jesus praying this prayer in the past? Why or why not?

What emotions do you think Jesus was feeling when He prayed "Thy will be done"?

Submitting to God's will over your will can be tough—and Jesus knows this better than any of us. He sent the Holy Spirit to help guide us. With the help of the Spirit and the tools mentioned earlier, God helps us do His will.

As we pray this petition of the Lord's Prayer, we are asking the Father for help and saying that we earnestly want to pursue His will for our lives no matter what the cost.

NOTES

Reflect

Think of a big decision that might come your way one day. How would the four questions on the previous pages help make things clearer?

Think of someone in your life who is a good example of following God's will no matter what the circumstances might be. Why did you think of this person?

The Small Catechism says God's will is done with or without us, so why is it important for us to pray "Thy will be done"?

In what parts of your life (mind and heart) do you need the Holy Spirit to help you work so that your prayer is "Thy will be done" instead of "my will be done"?

Read

JOHN 6:40

How does this verse line up with our definition of God's will?

1 THESSALONIANS 4:1–7

How would you summarize what Paul says God's will is?

What are some things in our world that God doesn't want to happen according to these verses?

Pray

Reflect on God's will for your life, and add your prayer requests. Clear away distractions, and just think about those things. Now use the space below to talk with God. **Write the prayer that comes to mind.**

To the One Who Knows Better Than I Do,

. . . In the name of Jesus. Amen.

NOTES

NOTES

4.6 Satisfied and Fed

Give us this day our daily bread.

With these words, we are asking God to give us what we need and letting that be enough. It's a tough thing to pray for just enough and nothing more. We are constantly surrounded by stuff—not just our stuff but everyone else's stuff too. We can find ourselves constantly wanting things, even if we don't necessarily need them.

So Jesus gives us these words as a reminder that God provides everything we need. He provides for all of our physical needs as well as our spiritual ones. He provides everything we need to be physically and spiritually satisfied and fed.

Here's another way to look at it: these words are a reminder for us to be **thankful, content, and thoughtful**.

- ☐ We are **thankful** because God freely gives what "bread" we need. He provides, and we lack nothing. For this, we're thankful.
- ☐ We are **content** because each day, God gives us exactly what we need. We don't have to worry about tomorrow. God will provide for our daily needs, and that's enough.
- ☐ We are **thoughtful** because as we use the words *us* and *our*, we are reminded that we are not the only ones who have daily needs. Through these words, God is also calling us to think of our neighbor and how they also have needs that can be met through the gifts He pours into our lives.

We may not always get what we want, but that's okay. Sometimes, God simply asks us to wait. When we do, He shows us what it means to depend on Him each day for exactly what we need—no more, no less. As we seek to be thankful, content, and thoughtful, we'll also find ourselves living each day satisfied and fed.

Reflect

Which do you think is hardest: being thankful, content, or thoughtful? Why?

What are your daily needs? See how many you can write down.

List some ways God could use you to help provide someone else's needs through the "bread" (whether spiritual or physical) He's already given to you.

Read

MATTHEW 6:25–34

What would you say is the main point Jesus is making?

What example does He give to reinforce that point?

What are the top three things people your age worry about? How does God provide for those worries?

NOTES

Pray

Take a few minutes to reflect on how God provides your daily bread (your spiritual and physical needs). Think about your prayer requests. Clear away distractions, and just think about those things. **Now use the space below to talk with God. Write the prayer that comes to mind. Fill every line!**

Great Provider of All That I Need,

. . . In the name of Jesus. Amen.

4.7 Forgiven and Forgiving

Forgive us our trespasses.

Have you ever owed someone a debt? For instance, have you ever borrowed $10 from someone and had to pay it back? Or have you ever broken something that belonged to someone else and it was your responsibility to replace it? No one likes being in debt. Sometimes, it just happens, and then it's our job to pay it back.

That word *trespasses* that we say in the Lord's Prayer is a word that means "sins" or "debts." You see, when we sin against God (or someone else, for that matter), it's as if we owe them something in return. We've done something wrong, and it cost that person something—now we have a debt to be paid or a wrong to be made right.

Here's our problem: **we owe a lot**. When it comes to God's Law and His will for our lives, we're daily racking up the bill. We owe more than we could ever pay back. Just spend a few minutes with the Ten Commandments, and you'll see pretty quickly how often we fall short and how much we owe.

That's where Jesus comes in.

Jesus' death canceled our debt.

Through the cross, our sins are no longer counted against us. Our debts have been paid! We owed a lot—more than we could ever pay back—and it was all completely forgiven through Jesus. Because of Jesus, we're able to pray this petition of the Lord's Prayer with honesty, humility, and confidence:

- ☐ We are **honest** with God, saying, "I know I am sinful, and I admit that I have broken Your law and have gone against Your will." God already knows our sin. In this petition, we're admitting that we know it too.
- ☐ We admit those sins with **humility**. We humble ourselves, recognizing that we are broken and sinful, and turn to God for His forgiveness.
- ☐ We ask God for that forgiveness with **confidence**. When we ask for God's forgiveness, we fully believe that God will forgive

NOTES

us—not because we deserve it but because through Jesus' death and resurrection, God guarantees it.

Each and every time we pray this prayer, we are reminding ourselves that we are asking God to forgive a debt that we could never pay back no matter how hard we tried or how long we lived. That's a pretty freeing feeling to know that such a big debt has been forgiven.

But this isn't just about us.

As we forgive those who trespass against us.

Because we have been forgiven, we forgive. This petition illustrates a pattern that develops in the Christian life that we'll call the "because, therefore" pattern. **Look up the verses below, and then draw a line from each of the verses to the "because/therefore" statement they correspond with.**

	BECAUSE . . .	THEREFORE . . .
Colossians 3:13	God has loved me,	I will love others.
John 13:34	God has been merciful to me,	I will be merciful to others.
James 2:13	God has forgiven me,	I will forgive others.

Before we wrap this lesson up, let's be clear about what it means to forgive someone. We forgive in the same way that Jesus does: immediately, fully, freely, and frequently.

- ☐ **Immediately**—When was the last time you went to church, confessed your sins as a congregation, and heard the pastor turn around and say, "Well, He'll forgive you, it'll just take some time." Never, right? Jesus doesn't wait one minute to forgive us; we shouldn't wait either. Restoration may take time, but forgiveness doesn't. Forgiveness is given immediately when it's requested.
- ☐ **Fully**—We forgive completely, not partway. Jesus doesn't look at your sin and only forgive a piece of it. He forgives all of it, so we do too.

NOTES

- ☐ **Freely**—The forgiveness we receive is free, so the forgiveness we offer is free. We should never find ourselves saying, "I'll forgive you if . . ." because Jesus puts zero stipulations on the forgiveness He gives to us.
- ☐ **Frequently**—How often should we forgive someone who keeps on sinning against us? As often as Jesus forgives us. We go back to Jesus all the time, asking for forgiveness when we mess up. He forgives us every time. It may hurt to forgive someone who keeps wronging you, but we do it because Jesus does the same for us.

This petition is a reminder for us to live our life each day with the certain confidence that we are forgiven and with a heart that truly desires to forgive.

Read

MATTHEW 18:21–35

What does this passage teach about being **forgiven**?

What does this passage teach about being **forgiving**?

Turn to Question 278 in your Small Catechism.

How does withholding forgiveness show we don't truly believe God forgives us?

NOTES

Reflect

Which is the hardest: forgiving immediately, fully, freely, or frequently? Why?

Why is it hard for some people to believe that they are forgiven fully and freely by God?

Do you have someone you need to extend forgiveness to? Include that need in your prayer.

Pray

Take a few minutes to reflect upon being a person who is **both forgiven and forgiving** along with your prayer requests. Clear your thoughts and just think about those things. **Now use the space below to talk with God.**

Merciful and Forgiving Father,

. . . In the name of Jesus. Amen.

4.8 Seeking Guidance

Lead us not into temptation.

Right on the heels of asking for forgiveness, we pray a petition for guidance. We are saying, "God, forgive me when I do wrong and guide me in the right direction when I'm being led down the wrong path." The trouble for us seems to be that going down the wrong path is a lot easier than we'd like it to be.

It's kind of like dominoes. Imagine a whole set of dominoes lined up in a row. If you knock one down, the next one goes, then the next one, then the next one. Temptation is sort of like that. Temptation is so easy, and the problem is that once we give in, we find ourselves giving in over and over and over again, and it feels like we can't stop it.

But we have good news! Here's what the Bible tells us:

> **No temptation has overtaken you that is not common to man. God is faithful, and He will not let you be tempted beyond your ability, but with the temptation He will also provide the way of escape, that you may be able to endure it.**
> **1 Corinthians 10:13**

This passage tells us, first, that **we are not alone**. Whatever temptation you are enduring, there are others who also have been through it or are going through it right now—chances are, you just haven't talked about it together yet! Second, God says you won't be tempted beyond what you're able to resist. That means no temptation is too great for you to overcome. Finally, God promises that when the time comes that you are tempted, He's always going to provide you a way out. You just have to look for it and actually want to follow where He guides.

NOTES

Read

MATTHEW 4:1–11

Did you know that Jesus faced temptation too? What is Jesus' weapon against Satan in this passage?

Satan's greatest weapon against us is a lie. Where does Satan twist the truth or outright lie in these verses?

EPHESIANS 6:10–20

God arms you as a soldier to fight against the enemy too! He doesn't leave you empty-handed as you head into battle. What do you think is the most helpful piece of the armor of God? Why?

Which piece (or pieces) of God's armor do you have questions about?

Faith Habit

NOTES

Back in Lessons 1.9 and 1.10, we introduced the idea of "Faith Habits for the Journey." These are habits that help every Christian grow in and nurture the faith that has been given to them in their Baptism. It's time to add in number three.

FAITH HABIT #3: RESIST THE ANCIENT ENEMIES.

In Lesson 4.5, we introduced three forces that are always acting against you as a child of God, working to lead you away from Him and His will for your life. We called them the "unholy trinity": the devil, the world, and our sinful flesh.

These three have been the enemies of God's people since the time of the fall, when the serpent tempted Eve and Adam to take the fruit from the forbidden tree (Genesis 3). As we learned in Ephesians 6, God has equipped us to resist them.

It's always good to know your enemies. If you know them, you have a better shot at beating them the next time it's time to combat them. Since these are the main culprits that tempt us into doing things we know we shouldn't do and going down the wrong path, let's spend a little more time identifying them.

- ☐ We can't dismiss the fact that **the devil** is the enemy of God and God's people. He will use all his power to try and pull us away from God. The main way he does that? A lie.
- ☐ The term ***the world*** is used often in the New Testament to describe the sinful environment that exists all around us. This is an environment that is at odds with God's kingdom and His will for you.
- ☐ Our **sinful flesh** is just what we prayed about in the previous petition. This is the part of us that is stuck with original sin and can't break the habit of actual sin (terms we will break down later).

Submit yourselves therefore to God. Resist the devil, and he will flee from you.
JAMES 4:7

Always remember the weapons that God gives you to resist these enemies. He has not left you alone, nor will He ever allow you to endure more than you can handle.

NOTES

Reflect

Why does it sometimes feel like there's no way out of temptation?

What are the greatest temptations people your age face?

Have you noticed temptations becoming more complicated as you've grown older? Explain.

Have you experienced God's power in helping you stand up to those temptations or known someone who has? Describe.

Pray

Take a few minutes to reflect on **how God guides you away from and protects you from temptation**. Think of prayer requests. Just think about those things. **Now use the space below to talk with God.**

My Leader and Protector,

. . . In the name of Jesus. Amen.

4.9 Without Fear

Deliver us from evil.

Every Christian faces a real battle with a real enemy. We cannot lose sight of this. When we take an honest look at this world, we see that while there is so much good, there is also evil—and plenty of it—mass shootings, genocide, terrorism, wars, poverty, hunger. While we may not see these things every day, these are very real issues that are still prevalent all over our world.

Satan is at the helm of all of that evil. So when we pray this petition in the Lord's Prayer, we are asking that God deliver us from both evil and the evil one.

As we talked about in the last lesson, Satan's greatest weapon against us is a lie. But it also helps to know his number one lie:

Satan's greatest lie is that he isn't real.

When we take a good look around our world, we learn the truth. He's alive and well and causing all sorts of evil anywhere that he is able. His goal is to deceive and destroy the human race. Why? Because as human creatures, created in the image of God, we are the crown of God's creation.

Since we are the crown of God's creation—the thing that means the most to God, enough that He sent His Son to die for us—and since Satan is God's number one enemy, we are Satan's number one target.

Even though all of this talk about evil and the evil one can be a little scary, we don't have to be afraid.

Christ's death and resurrection have freed us from Satan's tyranny.

Satan has no power over us—it was all taken away from him on that very first Easter. You and I can live without fear because of the victory we have in Jesus Christ.

For more information and Bible verses about Satan, head over to Question 287 in your Small Catechism.

NOTES

Read

How might the following verses help you when you experience evil? Write your answer beside them.

PSALM 46:1–3

DEUTERONOMY 31:6

PSALM 91

2 TIMOTHY 4:18

Reflect

What are some things people identify as causes of evil in our world?

How does God show us what is good and what is evil?

What would life without evil look like?

What advice would you give to someone who is very afraid of evil? What sort of things could they do when they're afraid to help them?

Pray

Take a few minutes to reflect on **how God delivers you from evil**. Think of prayer requests. Just think about those things. **Now use the space below to talk with God.**

Great Deliverer,

. . . In the name of Jesus. Amen.

NOTES

Unit 4 Reflection

We began this unit and began each lesson with the reminder that when you pray the Lord's Prayer, each petition is reminding you of your Father's goodness and mercy, strengthening you to live your life in such a way that you daily receive His gifts and commend your life to Him.

Which petition of the Lord's Prayer helps remind you most to daily receive God's gifts? Why?

Which petition helps you most to daily commend your life to Him? Why?

What is most important to you about the practice of prayer (not just the Lord's Prayer but actually talking with God)?

How has your understanding of the Lord's Prayer changed or deepened after working through this unit?

Pray

Time to write one final prayer for this unit. **Take a few minutes to reflect upon all the words of the Lord's Prayer, as well as your prayer requests.** Clear away distractions, and just think about those things. Use the space below to talk with God. **Write the prayer** that comes to mind. Fill every line.

,

. . . In the name of Jesus. Amen.

NOTES

NOTES

You have completed Unit 4.

Complete your Unit Check-In.

NOTES

Unit 5

How Do I Interact with God and How Does God Interact with Me?

PART 1

You've tackled some big questions so far: What does it mean to follow Jesus? Who am I? Who is God? How do I live my life? You've taken a look at the Bible, the Ten Commandments, the Apostles' Creed, and the Lord's Prayer. In the next three units, we're going to be tackling another major question—this one with two parts:

How do I interact with God and how does God interact with me?

Sometimes God can seem distant. When we read His Word, however, we get a different perspective. As we read through the Scriptures, we see how God's main desire is to have a relationship with His creation—especially His people. He walked with Adam and Eve in the garden, He journeyed with the Israelites through the wilderness, He dwelled in the temple in Jerusalem, He sent His Son to dwell with us in the flesh, He poured out His Holy Spirit over His people to dwell with them in a new way, and in Revelation, God says that He will dwell with His people forever.

So why does God sometimes seem so distant today? Has He abandoned us, or is it possible that He is still very present in our lives, working all around us even when we don't always see it?

That's what we get to explore in these next three units. First up for us is something that may seem pretty familiar to you. After all, it's something we see often in church and talk about often as Christians. Even so, it's a very real and present way that God interacts with each and every one of us. He calls us by name, covers us in His Word, and gives us a promise that can never be taken from us.

In this unit, we're talking about **Baptism**.

NOTES

5.1 The Means of Grace

Imagine you have to get a gift for someone. Let's say it's a pretty special gift. You have thought a lot about what you want to give to this person and you've found the perfect gift. You've gone to the store, you've ordered it online, or maybe you've made it yourself—whatever way you're imagining it, you've got the gift sitting in your room, and you have to decide what to do with it.

Another way to think about the Means of Grace is to think of them like a delivery truck! The delivery truck is not the package, it's just the way the package gets to where it's going. In the same way, God delivers His grace to us through His Word and His Sacraments.

How will you give the gift? You could just hand it to the person just the way it is—that would work, sure, but this gift is very important to you. This is no ordinary gift! You want to make sure the person receiving this gift knows that too. You decide to put it into a special box. You make it look nice! After all, it deserves a little extra attention.

God has a pretty big gift to give us too: **His grace.**

Have you ever really thought about what grace is? **Grace is the free gift that God gives to us because of what Jesus accomplished for us on the cross.** Another way to think about grace is by this acronym:

God's Riches At Christ's Expense

That's **grace**. God gives to us His riches (forgiveness of sins, eternal life, and salvation), and it costs us nothing—there is no expense for us to pay because Christ already paid it. God's riches at Christ's expense—that's grace in a nutshell.

So if God has this great gift to give us, how does He deliver His gift? In what way does He choose to wrap His gift up for delivery? Scripture shows us that He does this through what we call the **Means of Grace**. Just like a gift box is a means, or a way, of delivering a great gift, God has His own ways, or means, of delivering His gifts to us.

As we look through the Scriptures, God has chosen to deliver His grace primarily through three means, or ways.

When we talk about the Means of Grace, we are talking about the Word and the Sacraments.

NOTES

In other words, when you think of how God chooses to deliver His grace, think of His Word and Sacraments as the gift box for the greatest gift He could give to us.

As we participate with God's Word and His Sacraments (Baptism and the Lord's Supper), God delivers His grace—that is, the riches of forgiveness, eternal life, and salvation all at Christ's expense. As you'll read in your Small Catechism (Question 292),

> These Means of Grace are not simply information presented for our consideration, but are God's Word doing what it says and actually giving and delivering to us what it promises.

In other words, the Means of Grace are God's response to the two-part question that we'll be focusing on for Units 5, 6, and 7: How do I interact with God and how does God interact with me? Through the Means of Grace. When we engage with God's Word, when we're baptized, and when we participate in the Lord's Supper, we aren't just reminding ourselves of God's promises of forgiveness, eternal life, and salvation—God is actually giving us those gifts in that moment.

NOTES

Reflect

Turn to question 292 in your Small Catechism and read the question and its answer.

According to what you read, what is the Gospel?

The Word is one of the Means of Grace. According to what you read, what do we mean when we say "the Word"? (*Really reflect on this one!*)

Use the margin of this page or the space below to **write down at least one question you have** from what you read in your Small Catechism.

Share this question with a parent, a pastor, or your confirmation mentor!

5.2 The Sacraments

In the first lesson of this unit, you learned that the Means of Grace include God's Word and the Sacraments. That second word, *sacraments*, might be an unfamiliar one to you—and that's okay! This journey is all about exploring things that might be unfamiliar to you and helping you grow in your understanding of what they mean.

Let's start with a simple definition for *sacrament*:

> **When we speak of a sacrament, we are talking about a holy act; something sacred or set apart.**

That sounds like a pretty broad definition, doesn't it? We'll narrow it down in just a moment. In the meantime, reflect on what that definition means. When we participate in the Sacraments, that time is holy—set apart—and unlike anything else. Why? Because God is present. God is interacting with us and we are interacting with Him. That's a pretty big deal.

Take a moment to **write at least a few sentences** about what it means to you that God would set aside certain times and places to interact directly with you.

Now let's turn to a more specific definition of what a sacrament is.

NOTES

Turn to Question 293 in your Small Catechism and use this question and its answer.

Fill in the following chart with the three key traits of a *sacred* or *set apart* act that we would identify as a sacrament:

Three Key Traits of a Sacrament

_______________ ***by the command of Christ;***

in which Christ joins His Word of promise to a _______________ _______________***;***

by which He offers and bestows the _______________ ***of*** __________ ***He has earned for us by His suffering, death, and resurrection [also known as a Means of Grace].***

With those key traits in mind, you might be asking the question "So how many sacraments do we have?" That's a great question! It's a question Christians have been asking since the time of the Reformation.

Using this criteria, we can identify two obvious sacraments: Baptism and the Sacrament of the Altar, also known as the Lord's Supper.

Since we are focusing on Baptism for this unit, let's take a look at how Baptism meets all three criteria:

Instituted by Christ—Turn to Matthew 28:19 and write it in the space below. This is where Jesus institutes, or establishes, Baptism in Scripture.

Visible element—What is the visible element that God attaches to His Word in Baptism? **Fill in the blank.** If you need help, check out Question 294 in your Small Catechism.

Baptism's visible element is _______________.

Offers forgiveness (Means of Grace)—How do we know Baptism gives us God's forgiveness? That's a great question to ask! **Turn to Acts 2:38 in your Bible and write it in the space below.**

These words guarantee that forgiveness is given to us in our Baptism. This is where Baptism is identified as a Means of Grace, a way in which God gives His forgiveness.

Baptism unites the Word with the water in a holy act commanded by God, through which He promises the Holy Spirit, the forgiveness of sins, and many other blessings. Through those gifts, the Holy Spirit renews all who are baptized.

Read

Take a look at Question 295 and its answer in your Small Catechism.

Why do we consider Baptism to be so important when all it seems to be using is something as ordinary as water? What makes it so special and why?

Think about some other places in Scripture where God's Word is shown to be powerful and **write them in the space below**. If you're struggling to think of some, search "the power of God's Word verses" online for some inspiration.

NOTES

If you're struggling to find the answer, look for the word that is used five times in the answer to Question 296.

Now look at Question 296 and its answer in your Small Catechism.

According to what you read, what is the important thing that needs to be present when we witness and participate in the Sacraments?

Why do you think this is important?

Reflect

We'll continue to explore these three key traits of a sacrament in this unit and the units to come. In preparation, **reflect on these three traits and ask yourself** why you think each of these is important or helpful when we think about the Sacraments.

Why do you think it's important that Baptism is instituted by Christ?

Why do you think it's important that Baptism has the visible element of water attached to it?

Why do you think it's important that Baptism is one of the Means of Grace, that is, that in Baptism your sins are forgiven and God gives you His grace?

5.3 So What Is Baptism?

After Jesus' resurrection and before His ascension, Jesus leaves His disciples with some pretty important words and instructions. Matthew records this moment:

> **And Jesus came and said to them, "All authority in heaven and on earth has been given to Me. Go therefore and make disciples of all nations, baptizing them in the name of the Father and of the Son and of the Holy Spirit, teaching them to observe all that I have commanded you. And behold, I am with you always, to the end of the age." Matthew 28:18–20**

These are the last words that Matthew records Jesus speaking to His disciples. We call this Jesus' **Great Commission**. It's Jesus telling His disciples what to do once He ascends: make more disciples, baptizing them and teaching them. With these words, Jesus is telling us that there's something to this thing we call Baptism. It's not just a nice thing we do—it's a command of Jesus that we follow.

Chances are high that if you're reading this, you've either been baptized or seen a Baptism in person. Maybe you or the person you saw being baptized was a baby or maybe you or they were older. Either way, each time we witness someone being baptized, it can serve as a great reminder of the same thing that was done and said to us. No matter what your experience with Baptism has been, I hope we can all agree on at least one thing: Baptism is important.

As we talked about in the first two lessons of this unit, Baptism is both one of the Means of Grace (a way in which God delivers His gift of grace) and a sacrament (or a holy act). This means that Baptism isn't just a nice, cute moment during a church service! It's a sacred act where God comes to us and does something incredible.

In order to get to the heart of what Baptism is and what it does, let's first get to the heart of what Jesus did for you. To do that, I want you to imagine a friend of yours asking this question: "What's the big deal about Jesus?"

What would you say?

NOTES

If I had to guess, I would say most people would say something about how Jesus saved you from your sins, His promise of eternal life, or His forgiveness. In other words, we'd talk about grace! Grace makes Jesus a big deal.

Because of Jesus' death and resurrection, we no longer have to pay the cost for our sins. Jesus already did that. Remember our definition of grace? God's riches at Christ's expense! Grace is a free gift we receive because of what Jesus has done.

So here's the ultimate question that comes to mind when we talk about Baptism:

How do I know that the grace God offers has been given to me?

What do you think? If that same friend who wanted to know why Jesus was such a big deal asked you the question above, how would you answer? **Take your time and write your answer** in the space below.

This is a really important question many people wrestle with throughout their lives. Some people wrestle with whether God's grace is for them because they believe they simply aren't good enough to receive God's grace. They may tell themselves they haven't worked hard enough for it, they've done too many bad things and they don't deserve it, or that God wouldn't give His grace to someone with so many doubts. As you can imagine, that's a really tough place to be. So where can someone feeling this way find hope?

When we turn to God's Word, He provides that hope:

These are key verses for Christians when we talk about God's free gifts of grace and faith!

For by grace you have been saved through faith. And this is not your own doing; it is the gift of God, not a result of works, so that no one may boast. Ephesians 2:8–9

God's gift of grace is just that—a gift! It's not based on our works or ourselves but in what Christ has done. We don't deserve this gift, but He gives it to us freely without any cost to us.

And how does He give us this incredible gift?

That's right! Through the Means of Grace: His Word and the Sacraments. How do I know that the grace God offers has been given to me? Because of what He has done, is doing, and continues to do through His Word and Sacraments. **It's not what I've done; it's what He does.** God continues to work through the Means of Grace to give us a concrete reason for the hope that we have.

Baptism is one of the most concrete of those reasons. Baptism is not about what we've done, because in Baptism, God is doing all the work! **Baptism is God pouring out His gifts of faith and grace to us through the water and His Word.**

Turn to page 285 in your Small Catechism and look at the answer to the question "What is Baptism?"

Fill in the blanks below with the words from that answer.

What is Baptism?

Baptism is __________ just plain ________________, but

it is the ____________ included in God's ________________

and _______________ with God's ______________.

Look up Question 298 and its answer in your Small Catechism.

Why do you think God so often uses ordinary things to accomplish powerful works?

Read Question 300 and its answer in your Small Catechism.

Using what you see here and learned in this lesson, what happens in Baptism?

NOTES

REMEMBER! When you're asked to look at a "Question" in your Small Catechism, it means to read through the question, answer, Bible verses, and notes!

NOTES

Read

TITUS 3:5–7

How do these verses connect God's work in Baptism to the salvation we have in what Jesus accomplished for us?

Reflect

Why is it important to remind ourselves that it's God's power that saves us, not anything we could do on our own?

How does remembering that God has given you forgiveness, life, and salvation through your Baptism help you to trust Him more?

5.4 A Slate Washed Clean

By now you've probably picked up on the fact that Baptism is a pretty incredible thing. In Baptism, God pours out His gifts of faith and grace at no cost to us through the water and His Word. If you've known about this for a while, then it might not take all that much for you to see why this is such a big deal.

For those new to faith or even those outside the faith, however, it might be a little harder to see why Baptism is a such a big deal. After all, what's the big deal about God giving us gifts? He seems like a pretty generous God. Why is it so surprising that He continues to be generous?

Turn in your Bible to read Luke 7:36–50. Summarize what you read in the space below.

When you think about the gifts God offers and gives to you in Baptism (grace, forgiveness, eternal life), which debtor in Jesus' story to Simon do you relate to more: the one who owed much or the one who owed a little? The reality for each and every one of us is that when it comes to what we deserve, we owe God a lot—more than we could ever repay.

Sin, in whatever form it takes, separates us from God. God wants nothing to do with what is wicked and evil. So you know what that means? We're all in trouble. Big trouble. Imagine someone has been keeping a list of every sin that you've ever committed. How long would that list be? Think about how long that list would be in just a week! All you have to do is look to the Ten Commandments to see how often you fall short of God's expectations for your life.

Because of that sin, there's a debt to be paid:

> **For the wages of sin is death.**
> **Romans 6:23**

NOTES

In other words, you don't deserve the grace that God gives freely. Rather, for even one of those sins on that list, we all deserve death—a spiritual, eternal death.

Now think about God's gift of grace, especially His forgiveness. Feels pretty good, right? Now keep in mind that even though He offers that gift of grace **freely to you**, it does come at a cost. It's just not a cost that you have to pay. It's been covered. It's been paid for. **Jesus paid that price for you**. Your slate is clean.

That phrase *clean slate* dates back to a time when people used chalkboards (made of slate) for a number of things. Maybe it was to work out problems in school or to keep track of what was owed at a store. If the problem on the board became too difficult to navigate or the debt was paid or forgiven, the slate chalkboard would be erased! A person would be given a new, fresh start because the board was cleared for them.

So how do I know that I have a fresh start? How do I know that my slate has been washed clean? How do I know Jesus paid the debt for me specifically? How do I know that the grace we've been talking about is for me? That's right: through the Means of Grace. **God wants you to know your slate has been made clean and He's the one that cleared it for you.**

So what does this have to do with Baptism? Let's start with the word:

The word *baptize* simply means to wash.

In Baptism, God has washed your slate clean. By delivering His grace to us through the water and His Word, He has washed away your sin. There's nothing left on the list that you owe. You have a clean slate! You have a fresh start. Your debt has been paid. In the same way soap and water take away the dirt from your hands, so in Baptism God's grace cleaned you up and washed away your sin.

God's desire for your life is that nothing would separate you from Him—so He did something about it. The debt was owed, He paid it for you. The old has gone, the new has come. Welcome to the new you!

Read

TITUS 3:4–7

According to verse 5, who saved you?

Why did He do it?

How did He do it?

What else does Paul say was poured out onto us (vv. 5–6)?

Now take a closer look at verse 7. What does Paul say was the ultimate purpose of what God has done? (Hint: We become something and gain something else.)

NOTES

NOTES

5.5 From Old to New

In the last lesson, you learned how God has cleaned your slate in Baptism. He has given you a fresh start—a new you! But maybe this question was running through your head as you were reading about God's promise to you in Baptism: if God has made me new and cleared my slate, why do I still sin? If my sins have been washed away, why is sin still a part of my daily life?

Here's the short version: it's in your genes.

Family trees are ways for us to talk about our ancestors, those who came before us in our family line. Some people can trace their family back many generations, but many people cannot. Tracing a family line can be helpful when looking at what health concerns might be genetically passed down from generation to generation, like heart disease or diabetes, and they're also fun to consider when you look at pictures and see physical similarities in appearance from one generation to the next. It's just the nature of how God designed things: parents pass things on to their children, who then pass things on to their children after that.

What would you say if I told you that we all come from the same family tree? It might not be much of a surprise to you if you think about what Scripture tells us. The human race all started with the same set of parents: Adam and Eve.

While they didn't pass on to everyone something like heart disease, diabetes, red hair, or blue eyes, they did pass something along to us that to this day every person has in common: sin. Sin is something that will, unfortunately, be with us until the day Jesus calls us to rest or the day Jesus returns and completes His mission of making all things new. Our first parents brought sin into the world, and from that day onward, sin has been passed down from one generation to the next.

This sinful reality for each of us is what we refer to as our **old Adam**. It's our sinful nature. It's why we sometimes confess in church, "We are by nature sinful and unclean." It's why David confesses in Psalm 51, "Behold, I was brought forth in iniquity, and in sin did my mother conceive me" (v. 5).

As we learned in our last lesson, that presents a problem to every person:

For the wages of sin is death . . .
Romans 6:23a

This is why Paul also writes:

For as in Adam all die . . .
1 Corinthians 15:22a

We've got quite the dilemma on our hands. We don't just need to change our family tree—the whole thing is dead from the start. We need an entirely new one! We need a new Adam to replace our old one, but, spiritually speaking, we're dead. We're incapable of making the change ourselves.

In Christ, we are taken from death to life. Spiritually speaking, we were born into sin—dead from birth. It's in our genes. The old Adam is something that has been passed down to us. Through Christ's death and resurrection, Jesus has made a way for a new family tree to take the place of our old one. He has become the new Adam. In Baptism, something incredible happens: **we are united with Jesus**. We are given a new head of the family tree.

Scripture talks about this often. **Write out the following verses completely** in the spaces provided below:

ROMANS 6:23

1 CORINTHIANS 15:22

COLOSSIANS 2:12

ROMANS 6:4

NOTES

In Baptism, you have been united with Christ, both to His death and to His resurrection. That means that in Baptism you died. And that's good news! The old Adam has been killed. The new Adam, Jesus, has taken his place. Because Jesus, the new Adam, has become part of your identity, you are also a "new man," made new in Christ. You've been born again! God has changed your family tree. He has taken you from Adam's tree of sin and death and replaced it with Jesus' tree of salvation and life.

Read

ROMANS 6:1–14

What is different about you now that you are baptized? **Use at least two full sentences to answer** this question.

Reflect

Turn to Questions 319, 320, and 321 in your Small Catechism.

Explore the questions, answers, and verses thoroughly. Using what you read in Romans 6:1–14, as well as the questions and answers from your Small Catechism, **fill in the boxes** below:

DESCRIBE THE OLD ADAM	
DESCRIBE THE NEW MAN	
DESCRIBE HOW THE OLD ADAM AND THE NEW MAN INTERACT WITH EACH OTHER	

Scenario

Your friend Nicky has never really been to church but has recently been looking into things about Christianity. Knowing you go to church, one day Nicky stops you in the hallway to ask you a question. Nicky says, "Hey! I've been looking into this Jesus stuff recently, and I keep coming across the phrase *born again,* but I'm not really sure what that means. How can someone be born again? We're already alive. How can someone be born a second time?"

How would you respond to Nicky?

NOTES

PARADOX: A statement that contradicts itself but is true at the same time.

5.6 Saints and Sinners

As you may have picked up in the last few lessons, there's a paradox at work in the life of a Christian that we need to appreciate in order to live out our baptismal promises every day:

Followers of Jesus are sinners and saints at the same time.

As we talked about in our last lesson, we all have this reality of a sinful nature that has been passed down to us by our very first parents. We're in a bit of a bind. We are by definition sinners. It's impossible for us to stop sinning completely, no matter how hard we try. At the same time, we've been forgiven and we want to live in that newness of life that Jesus brings us. We've been made right by Jesus, which makes us saints, holy and set apart. But we still sin. But Jesus forgives us. And we sin some more. And Jesus forgives us all over again. Sinners and saints at the same time.

So where does Baptism come into play with all of this? As you saw in Romans 6, Paul gives us a pretty graphic picture of what happens in Baptism. Here it is again:

> **What shall we say then? Are we to continue in sin so that grace may abound? By no means! How can we who died to sin still live in it? Do you not know that all of us who have been baptized into Christ Jesus were baptized into His death? We were buried therefore with Him by baptism into death, in order that, just as Christ was raised from the dead by the glory of the Father, we too might walk in newness of life. Romans 6:1–4**

Paul's description of Baptism here in Romans 6 is a description of the daily struggle that we all face. In your Baptism, your old, sinful self is put to death and your new, righteous self is brought to life. As a baptized child of God, whom Christ died for, that baptismal dying and rising is something you will experience every day until Jesus returns or calls you to rest.

Until then, we live in that tension between the reality that our Baptism allows us to call ourselves saints—truly and concretely forgiven and saved—and the reality that we still fall short in our sin.

Read

Romans 6 isn't the only place Paul talks about this baptismal reality of putting to death the old Adam and being raised to new life with Jesus. **Turn to Colossians 3:1–10 and read it a few times.** Feel free to **highlight or make notes** about things that you feel are important as you read.

After you've read it a few times, **draw a picture or write a poem** in the space below that depicts our daily putting our old Adam to death and rising to the new life we have in Christ.

What comes to mind when you think about this tension of being both a saint and sinner at the same time? **Draw that!**

NOTES

Want to read more about how Baptism is a picture of the Christian's daily life? Check out Question 322 in your Small Catechism.

Scenario

You've been going to church with Thomas since you were little. You haven't seen him at church in a while though. One day while you're talking with him at school, you ask him why you haven't seen him at church lately. He says, "I used to feel close to God and really knew that He loves me. But I've done some really bad stuff lately, and I haven't been praying or reading my Bible or going to church. I don't know . . . what if I'm too far away from Him? I feel like I have to do something to get my faith back so I can be sure that I've even got a chance at heaven. What should I do?"

Knowing that Thomas is baptized, what would you say to him? **Use at least three complete sentences** to respond.

Faith Habit

This tension that we live in brings us to our next faith habit:

FAITH HABIT #4: REMEMBER YOUR BAPTISM.

Remember, these faith habits are those practices that help every Christian to grow in and nurture the faith that has been given to us in our Baptism.

How important do you think it is for us to remember that our salvation is taken care of? That's why God gave us this gift of Baptism. He wanted us to know concretely that what Jesus did for us on the cross and in His resurrection was all that we needed. He wanted you to know that His promise was for you, so He called you by name in Baptism as His name was spoken over you: Father, Son, and Holy Spirit.

That's why it's also important to take the time to remember your Baptism. Every day, your Baptism serves as a reminder that Jesus' promise of forgiveness, life, and salvation is true despite your tendency to sin. Baptism has united you with Jesus. **His promise covers you.** It wasn't based on something you did or didn't do but on what Jesus has done. You are eternally clothed with Christ. **That's a promise you carry with you every single day.**

Being a baptized child of God, whom Christ died for, means you and I are able to be honest about being sinful. Because of what Jesus has done for us, that sin no longer defines us. Daily you have the privilege to remind yourself of the baptismal promise that you are forgiven and free.

People choose to remember their Baptism in a number of ways! Here are a few suggestions as you continue your journey and seek to daily remind yourself that God's promise to you in your Baptism is enough:

- ☐ How often do you **wash your hands**? I hope it's a lot! Remember that the word *baptize* simply means to wash—every time you wash your hands or take a shower can be a reminder of God's baptismal promises to you!
- ☐ Have you ever seen someone **make the sign of the cross** over themselves in church? It's typically done when the pastor says God's name: Father, Son, and Holy Spirit. At these words, the sign of the cross helps us remember our Baptism.

NOTES

Those are the same words said over each of us in our Baptism as the pastor made the sign of the cross upon our head and upon our heart.

- ☐ Celebrate your **baptismal birthday**! Put it on the calendar, and do something special the next time it rolls around. It's worth celebrating God's gift to you!

5.7 Welcome to the Family

Have you ever noticed that after someone is baptized, the congregation is invited to welcome that person into the family? It's a great moment of celebration for the Church—not just those gathered in that space but the Church throughout the world. Our family grows just a little bit bigger every time someone is baptized.

That word *Church* is often referred to as the Body of Christ! It's not a building, it's the people. As believers, we are united together in Baptism as the Church because we are all united to Jesus in Baptism.

Now some might wonder: aren't we already in the family? Aren't we already all creations of God? While, yes, it's certainly true that God loves each and every person because they are all His creations, God has established Baptism as one of those concrete ways that He brings people into the family of faith. In Baptism, we are united to Christ's death and resurrection through faith. Through that faith, given to each and every Christian, God gathers this family that we call ***the Church***.

So if Baptism brings us into the family, what is our reality like before Baptism? In his Letter to the Galatians, the apostle Paul describes the difference between life before and after Baptism as being like the difference between a slave and a son. Back when Paul wrote this letter, families would often have servants or slaves who would spend their whole lives in servitude to a household. If you were one of those slaves, you certainly were a part of the household but not in the same way that a son was a part of it. A son had rights that a slave simply didn't have.

Put yourself into their shoes by imagining you were either a slave or a servant back in Paul's time. **List two differences** between slaves and sons in the space below.

Jesus came to set the captive free. Jesus died and rose again so that we would be freed from our slavery to sin and brought into His

NOTES

family. In Baptism, God delivers His gift of grace that sets us free once and for all. Before Baptism, it would be easy to see God as a master rather than a Father. Similarly, before we became united with Christ in Baptism, there was no way to know things like peace, freedom, and hope—we were slaves. Now God calls us His children.

The next time you witness a Baptism, I hope you're reminded that at some point that was you being freed and welcomed to the family. I hope it's a reminder to you that you are never alone, that God has surrounded you with brothers and sisters across this world, and that you have a Father who has gone to great lengths to show His love for you. You've been adopted into the family once and for all.

Read

GALATIANS 3:19–4:7

Now **read it a second time out loud**. Keep it open as you complete the questions below.

In 3:22, what does Scripture say we were imprisoned under before Baptism?

In that same verse, what is the reason given for the promise?

What does 3:27–29 say about Baptism?

How does 4:6–7 connect to Baptism?

Reflect

NOTES

If every Christian reminded themselves that we are all brothers and sisters in Christ, what would the Church look like? How would we treat one another? What would be different? What would be the same?

As baptized Christians, belonging to Christ, we are all heirs according to the promise given in our Baptism. How is the promise given in Baptism like an inheritance that is given to an heir?

What does life as a child of God—a member of the family—look like?

NOTES

5.8 Confirming Your Baptism

As we come to the close of this unit on Baptism, it's important for us to return to something we talked about all the way back in the very first lesson of Unit 1.

What is this process we call confirmation all about?

This confirmation journey is an opportunity for you to grow deeper in the **faith** that was given to you in your Baptism. When you come to the end of this journey, you will stand before the congregation to publicly confirm the faith that was given to you in your Baptism as your own. **So what exactly is faith?** Faith is this gift from God that creates within each and every Christian a belief and trust in Christ alone.

One of the most important things we can remember about faith is that it is truly a gift. It's not something we've earned but something we've been given. Check out these verses from Scripture that help us to see this truth about faith:

> **And Peter said to them, "Repent and be baptized every one of you in the name of Jesus Christ for the forgiveness of your sins, and you will receive the gift of the Holy Spirit." Acts 2:38**

> **So faith comes from hearing, and hearing through the word of Christ. Romans 10:17**

> **For by grace you have been saved through faith. And this is not your own doing; it is the gift of God, not a result of works, so that no one may boast. Ephesians 2:8–9**

> **Therefore I want you to understand that no one speaking in the Spirit of God ever says "Jesus is accursed!" and no one can say "Jesus is Lord" except in the Holy Spirit. 1 Corinthians 12:3**

> **They said to Him, "What must we do, to be doing the works of God?" Jesus answered them, "This is the work of God, that you believe in Him whom He has sent." John 6:28–29**

With this gift of faith, we are able to find answers to these questions that we've been wrestling with throughout this journey: Who am I? Who is God? How should I live my life? How do I interact with God and how does God interact with me? Without faith, we would not be able to come close to an answer to any of these questions.

That's why it's so important for us to remember what this journey is ultimately about. God has given you this gift of faith. Maybe it first came to you when you heard the promises about Jesus from His Word, or maybe you were a baby when God placed His promise on you through the waters of Baptism and His Word that was spoken over you. Whenever it was, God has great things in store for you as you continue to grow in that faith and what it means for your life.

That's what this journey is all about. Your confirmation journey began at the font of Baptism, and it won't be ending on the day you are confirmed. On that day, you will publicly confess your ongoing baptismal faith as a part of God's bigger story of salvation in front of your family, friends, and fellow believers. You'll pledge your ongoing, lifelong faithfulness to Christ. What began at your Baptism will continue throughout your life until the day when Jesus returns or calls you to rest.

Reflect

Consider what your life will be like in five years. What would you like your faith to be like then? Would you like to remain faithful in the confession you will make at Confirmation—that your faith would be more important than your own life?

Write a note to yourself in the space below describing what you would like your faith and life to look like five years from now.

NOTES

NOTES

FAQs about Baptism

Your Small Catechism is full of some pretty incredible questions, answers, and Bible verses on this topic of Baptism. These two pages highlight a few of them. Explore your catechism for more!

If Jesus already won full forgiveness for us, why do we need Baptism? Great question! Jesus has indeed atoned for the sins of the whole world and reconciled the world to Himself. In Baptism, He gives to us personally the forgiveness of sins that He acquired for all of humanity so that we would not be lost in doubt wondering if His gift of forgiveness is for us. He calls us by name and His name is said over us so that we would have confidence in what He has done. For more information, check out Question 309 in your Small Catechism.

Do you have to be baptized to be saved? Nope! It is certainly possible for an unbaptized person to be saved. Only unbelief condemns. For example, before the institution of Baptism, Old Testament believers were saved through faith in the promise of Christ. However, faith does not despise what the Lord promises and gives in Baptism. Those who are not baptized should be encouraged to be baptized in order to receive the gifts God offers there in a very concrete and personal way. For more information, check out Question 312 in your Small Catechism.

Should I be rebaptized? If you have no record or certain knowledge of your Baptism, by all means speak with your pastor about the possibility of being baptized. He will be glad to help because God wants you to have the assurance of His promises that Baptism gives. If you have been baptized (and your are certain of it), remember that Baptism is God's work, not ours. God's work is sufficient—it does what it says. Sometimes we can be tempted to think that it didn't work, but remember that sometimes Satan tempts us to doubt God's work of salvation in our lives. If you're really struggling with this, be sure to talk with your pastor.

Is it possible for a baptized person to fall from faith and be eternally lost? Yes. It's true that God's promises in Baptism remain true even if we do not believe them. However, all who reject God's promises and die in unbelief have abandoned their Baptism and do not receive what God has promised. For more information, check out Question 313 in your Small Catechism.

Does infant Baptism count? You bet! Jesus said go into all the world and baptize "all nations." Infants are included in those words. We should also keep in mind that babies, like every person, are sinful by nature. It's in our spiritual genes. We all need what Baptism promises: the forgiveness of sins and the gift of the Holy Spirit. Finally, it's important to remember who is doing the work in Baptism—it's the Holy Spirit! Not us. Our God is pretty powerful and is able to work faith where He wills. For more information, check out Question 303 in your Small Catechism.

Are we to seek a "baptism with the Holy Spirit" in addition to Holy Baptism? Nope! The Holy Spirit works through the one Baptism instituted by Christ (see Ephesians 4:5). Christian Baptism is not a water-only or Spirit-only Baptism but a Baptism of water and the Holy Spirit (see John 3:5; Titus 3:5; and 1 Corinthians 6:11). For more information, check out Question 318 in your Small Catechism.

Is a Christian's faith in Baptism or in Jesus? Yes! A Christian's faith is in Jesus *and* in Baptism because Jesus has put His Word of promise in the water. Faith takes hold of Christ where He has promised to be for us. To trust in your Baptism is to trust in Christ, who saves us through the washing He has joined to His Word. For more information, check out Question 317 in your Small Catechism.

NOTES

Unit 5 Reflection

Now that you've worked through Baptism, it's time to reflect a bit on it as a whole.

Talk to someone who was baptized a long time ago (parents or grandparents are great, but any follower of Jesus in your life will do). **Ask that person the following questions and record his or her responses.**

When and where were you baptized?

Why is Baptism an important event in the life of a Christian?

What does it mean to you to be a baptized child of God?

Taking It Home

When were you baptized? How old were you?

Where were you baptized?

Were any special family traditions included? Did you receive any gifts? wear something special?

Did you have sponsors or godparents? If so, who were they?

Use complete sentences in your answer! Feel free to use the margin of the page to keep writing if you run out of room.

Now that you've taken the time to really dive into the meaning of Baptism, take a moment to reflect on this question: **What does your Baptism mean to you?**

As you close this unit, look up the words to a beautiful hymn about Baptism: "God's Own Child, I Gladly Say It." You can find it in a hymnal such as *Lutheran Service Book* (*LSB* 594). Search online for a recording if you'd like to listen to it.

NOTES

You have completed Unit 5.

Complete your Unit Check-In.

NOTES

Unit 6

How Do I Interact with God and How Does God Interact with Me?

PART 2

When we really start to think about what it means that God could interact with us and we could interact with Him, the thought can be a little intimidating. God is wholly other and set apart. He is holy, perfect, and pure. Sin has no place in His presence.

We, on the other hand, are completely different. When we really start to reflect on our lives, we see how far the distance really is between God's perfection and our sinful reality. Couple that reality with the thought of coming into the Lord's presence and you've got a recipe for anxiety.

Moses shares that anxiety as he steps into God's presence at the burning bush. In many of the psalms, David acknowledges the dreadful reality of the separation his sin caused between him and God. Isaiah is mortified as he stands in front of the throne of God fearing for his life as he recognizes that, as a sinner, he has no right to be in the presence of a holy and perfect God.

So what are we to do? How can we, as sinful human beings, interact with a God who is wholly different than we are and who wants nothing to do with sin?

If you've already started to reflect back on Jesus, then you're moving in the right direction. Jesus changed everything for us. Jesus took on the weight of our sin on the cross so that there would be no separation between us and God.

As we learned in our last unit, that's why Baptism is such a big deal. In Baptism, you were united with Jesus' death and resurrection. Your sin has been buried with Christ, and He invites you to new life every single day.

So where do we go from here? In this unit, we'll explore another opportunity God provides for us to receive His forgiveness so that we can live in the joy of our new, forgiven reality—the practice of **confessing our sins**.

NOTES

6.1 In the Beginning . . .

As you explored the truly incredible gift that we have each received in Baptism, you were introduced to the concept of sin and caught a glimpse of its consequences. As you turn the page and begin to explore this practice of confessing your sins and receiving forgiveness, it's time to take a closer look at sin and peel back its layers.

Let's start at the beginning.

In Genesis 3, we receive the origin story of how and when sin entered into the world. Keep in mind where it all started in Genesis 1. God created, and when He was finished, He called His creation good—not just good but very good.

> **And God saw everything that He had made, and behold, it was very good.**
> **Genesis 1:31**

This is the picture we get at the beginning. It's a perfect design!

If you were to read Genesis 1 without reading the rest of Genesis, you might look around and say, "Well . . . what happened? The world I live in is far short of a perfect design." That's what Genesis 3 helps us to see. In Genesis 3, we see sin enter into the world and break God's perfect design. Take a moment to open up your Bible and **read Genesis 3 before you continue**.

The passage you just read describes the moment when sin entered into this world and all the effects that came from its presence. After reading Genesis 3, how would you define sin?

When we're asked to define sin, we might say something like, "Sin is when you do something bad." I've found that may not be the most helpful way we can describe it. For instance, think about what you just read in Genesis 3. We know what Eve did was bad, but why do we know it's bad? Who gets to decide?

As you continue this unit and this confirmation journey, consider this definition of sin instead, especially as you reflect on what you read in Genesis 3:

Sin is anything that diverges from God's will.

There in the garden, in Genesis 2, we see God instruct Adam and Eve with just one direction: don't eat from the tree of the knowledge of good and evil. That instruction is God's will—it's His desire for His creation. God, who made all things, knows what's best for His creation. He knows how it was designed to function. When you and I depart from that design, from His instructions, we're sinning. We're falling short of God's original design. We break what God intended to be whole.

Genesis 3 tells us more about sin than we initially see. Consider these five lessons we learn about sin from the words you read in Genesis 3:

1. **Sin broke God's perfect design for His creation.** No matter how wonderful life in this world may seem at times, it's nowhere close to God's original design for His creation. Everything was affected by sin, even creation itself. Notice how thorns infested the ground as a result of the curse of sin!
2. **Sin separates us from God.** God's relationship with His creation was also broken. Adam and Eve hid from God as soon as He returned to the garden after Eve took the fruit. Sin had entered the world and separated them from God, causing them to hide. They strayed from His will, and they knew it.
3. **When confronted, we play the blame game.** Adam blamed Eve. Eve blamed the serpent. We often do the same thing when we're caught in our sin. We want to blame our sin on someone or something else. God invites us to be honest, however, claiming our own responsibility when we fall short

NOTES

of His will and design for our lives. When we do, He responds with forgiveness.

4. **Sin brings with it a very real curse: death.** As a result of Adam and Eve's disobedience, death entered the world. God's design of life for His creation broke, and with this brokenness came death—but a promise was given that this would not be the end result forever because . . .

5. **Restoration is God's goal.** In Genesis 3:15, God made a promise that He would send someone who would redeem and restore His creation. This One He would send would crush the serpent's head as His heel was bruised. He was speaking of Jesus. Satan received that fatal blow as Jesus took the punishment on the cross that we deserved for our sin: death. Why? Because we could not pay the price ourselves. We could never pay God the complete price that our sin demanded. We needed a Savior, and God sent us His Son.

As you continue to explore what it means to confess your sins, it's my hope that you'll remember that you aren't alone in your sins or your need to confess. Remember, we're all in the same family. Genesis 3 is a piece of our family history. We all come from the same line, which means we've all got sin in our spiritual genes. As the Bible tells us, we have all fallen short of the glory of God—that is, we've all broken His design as we've diverged from His will and instructions for our lives. But we also know that the free gift of God is eternal life in Christ Jesus.

That's why He invites us to confess those sins! As we confess, He forgives. It's one of the ways God interacts with us and we interact with Him.

Reflect

Someone might say, "Sin is when you do bad things." Why is that not the most complete explanation of sin? Where does that definition fall short?

Of the five lessons we learn about sin from Genesis 3 found on the previous two pages, which one do you think is the most important? Why?

Scenario

You're talking to your friend Heidi. She has come to the conclusion that it's silly how Christians still talk about Adam and Eve. She says, "Why don't we just talk about Jesus? I mean, that's the point of being a Christian. Why does the old stuff matter?"

What do you say? Why is important for us, as Christians, to remember and talk about Adam and Eve?

6.2 Original Sin and Actual Sins

Up to this point, we've talked a whole lot about the sin that we've inherited from our first parents, Adam and Eve. Meanwhile, we also have all of those sins that we've committed ourselves. So which ones are we responsible for, which ones make us guilty, and what's the right way to talk about all this sin?

These are all wonderful questions. To begin to answer them, let's start with an even better question that your Small Catechism asks on page 56. **Turn to Question 20 and fill in the blanks below.**

What is ______?

______ is humanity's fallen condition. We are turned away from ______ and unable to look to ______ for security, meaning, and righteousness. This inner ______ condition results in actual ______ of thought, desire, word, or deed that are contrary to God's will as summarized in the Ten Commandments.

Put more simply, we've got two types of sin that we need to recognize, and we're accountable for both: **original sin and actual sins**.

- ☐ **Original sin** is the sin we have inherited from Adam and Eve.
- ☐ **Actual sins** are those sins that we commit in our thoughts, our words, our actions, and our inaction.

We are covered in sins from head to toe. We were born into it, and because it has been a part of who we are since before we were born, we find ourselves living in it over and over and over, day after day ever since. We're stuck.

Because of original sin, we have been messed up and broken from the start. Meanwhile, because of our actual sins, we continue to mess up and become more broken.

This is why it is so important that we remember the promise that God made to humanity in Genesis 3:15, a promise that finds its fulfillment in Jesus Christ. **God would not leave us broken!**

NOTES

Jesus shows up and changes everything for us. Alone, all we have is our sin, which leads to death, which leaves us hopeless and in despair. But we're not alone, which means you're not alone. God sent Jesus to set us free, to remove what has separated us from Him, and to make good on His promise to bring restoration to His fallen creation.

Reflect

Which do you think is harder for people outside of Christianity to wrap their minds around: original sin or actual sins? Why?

What would be the danger of only talking about original sin and never talking about actual sins?

Similarly, what would be the danger of only talking about actual sins and never talking about original sin?

NOTES

Explore

Turn in your Small Catechism to page 57 and read the whole page as it explores the question "How does original sin affect every human creature?"

Do you find original sin helpful in understanding why bad things continue to happen in our world? Why or why not?

Do you find yourself embracing your identity as a sinner as you work through this unit so far, or resisting it? Why? Use full sentences to explain.

These would be great to ask a parent, guardian, mentor, pastor, or other trusted adult!

What questions do you find yourself asking about sin at this point?

6.3 So Is Anyone "Good"?

If you're one who is struggling to embrace your identity as a sinner, know you're not alone. In August of 2020, Arizona Christian University released the results of a research study they did with American adults.[1] They found that 48 percent of the adults they polled believed that "if a person is generally good, or does enough good things during their life, they will 'earn' a place in Heaven." Similarly fascinating, in that same survey, 69 percent of the adults surveyed said that they believed "people are basically good." Probably most interesting about the results was how many of those folks who agreed with these statements also considered themselves Christians.

Here's the thing: if getting to heaven is based completely on us being "good," then we really don't have a whole lot of hope. That's probably no surprise to you after the first couple of lessons in this unit.

Many times we're tempted to compare ourselves to others, to see whether we'd call ourselves "good." In reality, we're not discovering if we're "good" when we make these sorts of comparisons. We're only discovering if we're "better" than the person we're comparing ourselves to. But here's the thing:

Other people are *not* the standard that tells us if we're good or not. Only God's design can do that.

And God's Word is pretty clear about how we all line up when compared to His original design:

If we say we have no sin, *we deceive ourselves*, and the truth is not in us. 1 John 1:8

There is *none* who does good, *not even one*. Psalm 14:3; 53:3 (See also Romans 3:12.)

For *all* have sinned and fall short of the glory of God. Romans 3:23

So what does this mean? It means that even the best of us fall short of the standard God has placed in front of us, which is His original

1 https://www.arizonachristian.edu/wp-content/uploads/2020/08/AWVI-2020-Release-08-Perceptions-of-Sin-and-Salvation.pdf. Accessed October 25, 2020.

NOTES

design. This is why the Gospel of Jesus Christ is so important for us to cling to with all that we have.

But what is the Gospel of Jesus Christ? *Gospel* is a word that literally means "good news." When we talk about the Gospel of Jesus Christ, we're talking about the Good News that He brought and continues to bring into this world.

Let's start with what the Gospel is not:

The Gospel *is not* that Jesus came into this world to take us from being bad people to being good people.

As you search through the Gospels (the books of the Bible that share the accounts of the life and ministry of Jesus Christ), you won't find a whole lot of places where Jesus talks about taking people from bad to good, because that wasn't His purpose. He knew us well enough to know that if it took us becoming "good" for us to be worthy of the gift of eternal life He came to give us, then we'd never get there.

Instead, we find Jesus sharing incredible news with the people He meets, leads, and teaches. He shares with them that eternal life will be possible because of what He is doing and would do. As Jesus walked around in His ministry, He saw the effects of sin in the world. Sin kills. As we explored in Unit 5, Romans 6 shares with us that "the wages of sin is death." Spiritually speaking, we're dead before the Good News of Jesus Christ comes to us to bring us life. And that's the Gospel. That's the Good News: it's not that we can do something that earns us eternal life but what Jesus has done that accomplishes that for us. Put another way:

The Gospel *is* that Jesus came into this world to take us from death to life.

As you continue to grow and live in the world, you'll be tempted like so many to think that somehow you and I can become "good enough" to be loved by God and that somehow our "goodness" allows us to have the promise of eternal life. Nothing could be further from the truth we find in the Scriptures. The truth is that God is the one who is good, and it's His goodness we cling to, not our own. The Good News is not that we found a way to get to God; it's that He found a way to come to us.

Reflect

Use at least two sentences to explain this statement: "There is no such thing as a 'good' person."

As Christians, our claim is that God is perfect—not us. So why do you think we get mad or upset when we realize (or when someone else notices) we mess up, sin, or fall short? Why is it hard for us to come to terms with ourselves when we've done something bad?

NOTES

Scenarios

You're hanging out at the mall and you and your friends see someone passing out papers about Jesus. Your friend Amaris says, as she makes a face, "Ugh. Christians. They just want everyone to be perfect like they are!" Then your friend Bernard jumps in, "Yeah. They just want us all to behave like little angels. Can you believe them?"

What might you say?

Your friend Jonathan seems to beat himself up a lot. He doesn't think he's "good enough" (whatever that means). This comes up in conversation every time you talk about church. One time he says to you, "That's nice that you can go to church. Me? Well, I'm not good enough yet. I've still got a lot of stuff I need to take care of before I can go. I'm just not a good person, that's all. I need to get my act together before I join you for youth group or anything."

What would you say to Jonathan?

While over at your friend's house, you hear his mom say something that makes you uncomfortable: "Don't become one of those self-centered Christians. They think they're the only ones who are good! Meanwhile, there are plenty of Muslims and Jews and atheists who are doing so much more good for the world than any Christians I see. They're good people doing good things—but God's going to send them to hell?"

What might you say?

6.4 Two Parts of Confession

It's time for some honesty: confession can be a scary thought, especially when you're starting out. In the world you're growing up in, perfection seems to be the norm. In reality, as you've already discovered, perfection is the furthest thing from the norm. Only God is perfect; the rest of us fall very far from the standard of perfection. Nevertheless, in a world where everyone seems to be perfect, the idea of confessing to anyone the ways you've sinned can be very intimidating.

That's why it's good to remind yourself that

Confession has two parts.

To help you better understand what that means and why that alone would make confession any less scary, **turn to page 306 in your Small Catechism and fill in the blanks** below using the question "What is Confession?"

What is Confession?

Confession has ________________ parts.

First, that we ____________ our sins, and second, that we receive ________________, that is, ________________, from the ______________ as from God Himself, not ________________, but firmly believing that by it our sins are ________________ before God in heaven.

In other words, without absolution (which is another word for forgiveness), the work of confession that God invites us to do is not complete. Every time you confess your sins, you can guarantee what comes next: **forgiveness**.

Consider for a moment how you typically respond to someone who apologizes to you. Your friend walks up to you, says they are sorry, and you say what? "It's cool." "It's fine." While you're telling them things are "okay" between you when you respond that way, it still leaves things somewhat unsaid. Well, guess what God says every single time? "I forgive you." It's a clear response that leaves nothing unsaid.

And why does God have this response for us every single time? Because He has already covered the cost. He sent Jesus into this world out of His love for you. He did not want anything in all of creation—particularly your sin—to be a barrier between Him and you. So He invites you to get all of it out in the open and hear what He has to say about it: **He forgives you.**

We get all of those things out in the open as we confess our sins and, in turn, receive absolution. While you may be familiar with how we practice confession together as a congregation when we come together for worship, know also that God places certain people in your life whom you can confess to as well, namely your pastor and your parents. God knows our hearts. He knows we can be tempted to think that there are still sins we've confessed that are left unforgiven. That's why He places people like pastors, parents, teachers, and others as His representatives in our lives to share with us His words of forgiveness directly and specifically to us.

He also invites us as Christians to confess our sins against one another directly to each other so that we can find reconciliation in those relationships as well. As you can see, confession is a tool—it's a gift—that God invites us to participate in as often as we are able. Why? Because it brings with it freedom as forgiveness is shared.

The idea of confessing can seem scary because you're afraid of how the person who hears that confession will feel about you, whether it's a neighbor you've sinned against, a pastor, a parent, or even God Himself. That fear comes from one place: Satan. As Jesus shares with us, Satan is a liar and the only thing he can ever do to us is lie. **Here's the truth: God loves you, He forgives you, and there's nothing you could share with Him that would ever change that.**

Read

1 JOHN 1:8–9

Read these verses out loud.

What do you think John means when he says we "deceive ourselves" if we say we have no sin? How is saying we have no sin the same as lying to ourselves?

On a scale of 1–10 (1 being no comfort at all and 10 the most comfort you've ever known), how much comfort do you receive from verse 9 when it comes to the idea of confessing your own sins? Why did you give that number?

Reflect

Do you find the idea of confessing your sins to be more freeing or more frightening? Why?

Consider the words you just used to answer the question above. **Write a prayer asking God to continue to strengthen your trust in Him and His promises**, especially when it comes to Confession and Absolution.

NOTES

NOTES

Turn in your Small Catechism to pages 307–11.

Read the entirety of those five pages. Write six takeaways from these pages in the space below.

Scenario

Your friend Earnest comes to church with you one day. At school the next day, Earnest asks you about that "weird part toward the beginning of the service—the one where you had to . . . confess things." He says, "I thought that was just a Catholic thing."

What could you share with Earnest about Confession and why we do it?

6.5 Repenting and Turning

As you explored page 307 in your Small Catechism at the end of the last lesson, there was a word you would have discovered there that needs a little unpacking. That word is ***repentance***.

Repentance is a word closely connected with confession. In your Small Catechism, you read:

The Christian life is one of repentance.

As you look to Scripture, you'll find that word used over and over again across both the Old and New Testaments. It's an important word for God's people to consider as they consider what it means to live according to God's design. But what does *repentance* mean? Put simply:

Repentance is the act of changing one's path.

As it relates to confession and the Christian life, repentance is the act of using the mind that God has given you to recognize what you've done wrong and, in so doing, change your mind from being okay with the sin you've committed to regretting and rejecting it. Repentance takes you to the one place you can go to get rid of that sin for good. Repentance takes you to Jesus.

But there's a second piece to repentance. Maybe better said, there's something else that partners with repentance in the life of a Christian: turning. As we repent, we change our minds, and that change of mind moves us to change our actions as well. Let's take a look at two examples from the Book of Acts to help us see this clearly:

> **Peter to the crowds: "Repent therefore, and *turn back*, that your sins may be blotted out." Acts 3:19**
>
> **Paul before King Agrippa: "But declared first to those in Damascus, then in Jerusalem and throughout all the region of Judea, and also to the Gentiles, that they should repent and *turn to* God, performing deeds in keeping with their repentance." Acts 26:20**

NOTES

What Peter and Paul want their audiences to understand is that repentance leads to a change in direction, behavior, and action. When you repent, you turn from your sins and turn toward your God. Genuine repentance changes the way you think, which, in turn, changes the way you choose to act moving forward.

A life of repentance is one that continually turns from sin and toward God, His design, and His purpose for your life.

Faith Habit

This brings us to the next faith habit. Remember, these are those habits that help every Christian to grow in and nurture the faith that has been given to us in our Baptism.

FAITH HABIT #5: REPENT AND BE FORGIVEN.

As you can tell from this lesson, repentance is a default state for a Christian. As Christians, we look to Jesus at every moment of our day. We trust Him, we seek Him, we follow Him. As we do, we're reminded of the love for us that was demonstrated on the cross and the new life that He calls us to through His Word. A significant piece of what we see when we look to Him at every step is the price He paid for our sin. It is never lost on us what He came to do so that nothing would ever separate us from His love, which means it is never lost on us what our sin deserves.

For this reason, we spend our lives in a constant state of repentance and turning from our sin and toward our Savior. As you learned in the previous lesson, this means that we are also constantly on the receiving end of His forgiveness. With our confession comes His forgiveness—this is the case every single time.

As you consider your life beyond this confirmation journey, ask yourself:

How will I intentionally make space to repent and be forgiven?

Satan will continue to challenge you with his lies. He will tell you that something is unforgivable or too big to forgive; he will tell you that whomever you would talk to about your sin will judge you and treat you differently. This is why it is so important for each of us as Christians to make repentance an intentional rhythm of our life—so that we can continually be on the receiving end of God's grace as we hear the sweet words of forgiveness that God has in store for us.

As you consider what it will mean for you to make this a central habit in your life, ask yourself these questions:

- ☐ Am I ready to commit to weekly worship in God's house so that I can be in a place where I will regularly confess my sins to God and receive absolution?
- ☐ Is there anything I feel standing in the way of me confessing my sins out loud to my pastor in private? If so, what baby steps could I take toward making this a practice that I can become comfortable with?

Take some time in prayer asking God for strength and wisdom to make this a regular habit for your life beyond this confirmation journey.

Read

PSALM 51:1–4

Read those verses out loud or listen to them on your Bible app. Keep in mind that these are the words David wrote after being confronted by Nathan about having Uriah killed.

Which words or phrases tell you that David's mind has changed about how he felt about having Uriah killed?

Why did those words or phrases stand out to you?

Would you ever consider using these words when you think about your own sin? Why or why not?

NOTES

You can find these words on page 307 of your Small Catechism under Question 325.

Reflect

The Small Catechism explains Confession this way:

In Confession, we admit that our sins have offended God and are deserving of His eternal punishment.

Do you find it easy or difficult to be reminded that each of your sins offend God and deserve the punishment of eternal death? Why?

Scenario

You are sitting across from your friends George and Mindy at the park. George is really upset about something in his past. He feels like he really did something wrong. Mindy's advice is, "I really think you should talk to someone about it. Sounds like confessing what you've done to someone would help. Maybe to the person that you wronged, maybe to a pastor, or even to a friend—just so you can hear that you're forgiven." George says, "I dunno," then looks at you and says, "What do you think? How could that help me?"

What do you say? How might sharing help George?

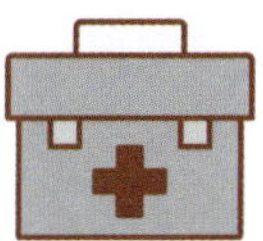

6.6 His Forgiveness

At the front of our church body's hymnal, *Lutheran Service Book*, you'll find the order for a service called "Corporate Confession and Absolution." This service is designed as an opportunity for a congregation to gather together for the sole purpose of confessing their sins and receiving absolution.

While the service itself is much shorter than most worship services you've probably been to, the words used for Confession are much more drawn out. It's designed to take the time to focus on and acknowledge what is actually happening when we come together to confess our sins and receive absolution. And what is happening? **We are interacting with God and He is interacting with us.**

But who is doing what? By now, I'm sure you'd say that's obvious. As for our part: we confess, we repent, we acknowledge our sin and ask for forgiveness. God then does what? **He absolves us! He forgives us.**

What's important about these moments where we receive forgiveness is this: we aren't just remembering that God forgives us, **God is actually forgiving us there in that moment.** That certainly becomes clear in this specific service of Corporate Confession and Absolution.

You see, while the confessional part of the service seems pretty similar—in that we all confess together a prewritten statement—the Absolution is done very differently. Everyone comes forward to receive the Absolution from the pastor individually at the altar, similar to how you might see people receive Communion individually. Each person approaches the altar to hear these words said specifically to them:

> **In the stead and by the command of my Lord Jesus Christ I forgive you all your sins in the name of the Father and of the Son and of the Holy Spirit.**

These words are said very intentionally.

- ☐ **"In the stead"** means that the pastor is standing in as a representative of Jesus, similar to how an ambassador of a country might speak in the place of the president of that country.
- ☐ Similarly, **"by the command"** is reinforcing that Jesus Himself has commanded this forgiveness to take place.

NOTES

Find these words on page 291 of *LSB*.

NOTES

- Finally, those words **"I forgive you all your sins"** are the words that have come from God Himself through the lips of the pastor in front of us.

God has given us this invitation to confess our sins and receive His forgiveness for a very specific reason: He knows we need it. We don't just need a reminder, we need His forgiveness—and He's willing to give it as often as we need it.

There's a specific line from this service of Corporate Confession and Absolution that I want to leave you with as you consider what it will look like for you to make Confession and Absolution an intentional rhythm that you participate in throughout your life. After the congregation confesses together, the pastor asks the congregation a very important question:

Do you believe that the forgiveness I speak is not my forgiveness but God's?

To which the congregation responds: **Yes.**

And the pastor replies: **Let it be done for you as you believe.**

A similar question is asked in "A Short Form of Confession" found on pages 312–13 in your Small Catechism.

The forgiveness we receive in church is not our pastor's forgiveness—it's God's. The pastor is not reminding you of God's forgiveness; God is actually forgiving you in that moment, interacting with you as you interact with Him.

Reflect

To explore more about how God has given this authority to forgive sins in His stead and by His command to His Church, **turn to John 20:19–23**.

What in this passage helps you to see that it is truly God's forgiveness that is being shared through His people?

NOTES

What does it mean to you that God actually forgives you in those moments when a pastor speaks the words of forgiveness to you?

For more on the forgiveness God shares through His Church, be sure to **check out pages 314–21 in your Small Catechism**.

NOTES

6.7 Some Final Advice

As we wrap up this unit on Confession, let's take a look at some practical first steps to take toward making this a lifelong practice. These pieces of advice will be great to return to whenever you find yourself struggling to get started or restarted with the practice of Confession.

As you're getting started, ask these two questions: How have I been doing at loving God? How have I been doing at loving my neighbor?

Back in Unit 2, we unpacked the Ten Commandments and saw how they help us answer the question "Who am I?" In the Ten Commandments, we discover that God designed each and every one of us to love Him and love our neighbor.

In this unit, we started off by acknowledging how sin is anything we do that strays from God's design. So, if we can summarize God's design for us by saying that we were created to love God and love our neighbor, then naming the ways we've sinned should be as easy as considering all the ways we've been unloving toward God and our neighbor. Simple, right?

Remember to consider every aspect of your life.

When it comes time to confess, it's important to remember that God already sees every aspect of your life. He sees you when you're at home, He sees you at school, and He knows about every moment when you're with your friends or by yourself.

It's easy to be tempted to compartmentalize God, but find comfort in knowing that God already knows what you're going to bring up as you confess your sins. Nothing is going to surprise Him, and nothing will make Him love you less. Every sin that comes to mind matters.

Make it a practice to actually name your sins and share anything that comes to mind—you'll find yourself with a clearer conscience.

Why does every sin that comes to mind matter? Because it's one more thing that Satan will try and use to make you believe you aren't worthy of God's love. This is why it's so important to share out loud to someone in confession. In response, you'll be able to hear a very specific forgiveness spoken aloud that addresses all those sins you cared to mention by name.

Martin Luther himself spent much time recounting his sins as often as he could. While his classmates would go in to confession and be out in a few moments, Luther was known to spend hours at a time confessing his sins. He took God up on His invitation to clear his conscience, as he received absolution for any and every sin that came to mind. The same can be true for you!

Make it a goal to always protect yourself from "cheap grace."

Whatever happens, always keep your eyes on Jesus. This will help you avoid "cheap grace." This is a term we use to refer to those times in life where we consciously acknowledge that what we're about to do is sinful but we do it anyway because we know God will forgive us for it in Jesus. This cheapens what God has given us. While it makes sin seem "not so bad" in the moment, we know the truth. Our sin is what took Jesus to the cross to experience the eternal punishment that we deserve.

What's the best way to avoid this habit of cheap grace? Be honest with someone God has placed in your life about the sins you commonly commit. They will help keep you accountable to honest repentance and a sincere effort to turn away from those sins and toward the life God has invited you to live.

Practice, practice, practice.

One of the most helpful things you can do is practice. Feel free to start small and see where God takes it from there. To get started, consider using these words as a daily prayer you can make your own over time:

> Heavenly Father, I know I have sinned. I haven't lived as Your child following Your ways. [Name the sins you can think of here.] I'm sorry for my sins and want to turn away from them, to stop doing them, and to live as a new creation. Because of Jesus, I ask for Your forgiveness, and I trust that in Your mercy You will forgive me. Thank You, God, for making me clean and new again. Help me live as Your child, following Your ways. In Jesus' name. Amen.

NOTES

NOTES

Read

PSALM 32:3, 5

Read those two verses out loud or listen to them on your Bible app.

In verse 3, David describes how his unwillingness to confess caused him physical pain. What does that tell you about the importance of confessing?

In verse 5, David gives in and confesses. What was the result?

Even though you know that withholding confession isn't healthy spiritually, physically, or mentally, and you know that God forgives every time you confess, what do you think will be the hardest piece of advice given in this lesson to follow? Why?

Unit 6 Reflection

NOTES

Now that you've worked through Confession, it's time to reflect a bit on it as a whole.

Talk to someone who has experience with confessing their sins regularly (parents or grandparents are great, but any follower of Jesus in your life will work). Bonus points if you can find someone who has gone to a pastor to confess!

Ask this person the following questions and record his or her response.

What do you remember about the first time you went to confess? Did you find it easy or difficult?

Why is Confession an important habit in the life of a Christian?

What about Confession and Absolution do you appreciate the most?

NOTES

Reflect

Time for you to reflect personally on Confession.

How has your understanding of Jesus' love for you changed or deepened after working through this unit?

What do you think is the most important thing people should know about Confession? Why?

What Bible verses specifically stuck out to you in this unit? Why did you find them so meaningful?

As you close this unit, look up the beautiful words of a hymn about Confession: *Lutheran Service Book* 616, "Baptismal Waters Cover Me." You can also search online to hear a recording. What words stand out for you?

NOTES

You have completed Unit 6.

Complete your Unit Check-In.

Unit 7

How Do I Interact with God and How Does God Interact with Me?

PART 3

When was the last time you interacted with God? I mean, you physically touched Him, saw Him with your eyes, and heard Him with your ears?

We're not talking about some mystical or spiritual experience. When was the last time you interacted with God the way Adam and Eve walked with Him in the garden? Or when Moses spoke with Him at the burning bush? Or as the Israelites did as they wandered with Him in the wilderness?

Never? Not surprising! While most of us would love to have that kind of interaction with God, the reality is we don't.

Jesus' words to Thomas at the end of the Gospel of John are important:

> **Have you believed because you have seen Me? Blessed are those who have not seen and yet have believed. John 20:29**

Fortunately for us, we fall into that second category of those who have not seen Him yet have believed. While we don't need to see God firsthand to define our faith, it does strengthen our faith and relationship with Him when we have something physical to connect to.

So God set in place a very special way for us to interact with Him in a very real way, physically receiving His grace and forgiveness. He instituted the Sacrament of the Altar (also known as Communion or the Lord's Supper).

God combines the power of His Word with the simple elements of bread and wine, and we receive forgiveness, life, the strengthening of faith, and connection with Him.

Psalm 34:8 declares,

> **Taste and see that the Lord is good!**

In the Lord's Supper, we get just that opportunity.

NOTES

7.1 Means of Grace Revisited

Back in lessons 5.1 and 5.2, we learned about the Means of Grace and the Sacraments. As we continue to dive a little deeper into the Lord's Supper in this unit, let's jog your memory on both of those since the Lord's Supper is both a Means of Grace and a Sacrament.

As you'll remember, the Means of Grace are how God brings or gives His grace to us. Just like when you wrap a great present in a beautiful box, the Means of Grace are the boxes for God's great gift of forgiveness, life, and salvation.

As we learned, looking through the Scriptures, we find that God has chosen to deliver His grace primarily through these means, or ways. **When we talk about the Means of Grace, we are talking about the Word and the Sacraments.**

God's Word was in our last unit, as we talked about the forgiveness God offers through His Word. Whenever God's Word is spoken or read, God is at work, bringing His grace to us.

We defined a sacrament as "a holy act; something sacred or set apart" and also laid out the three primary criteria that must be met in order for something to be considered a sacrament. Fill in the blanks below with the information about those three criteria. If you need help, refer back to Lesson 5.2 or Question 293 in your Small Catechism.

Three Key Traits of a Sacrament

__________________ *by the command of Christ;*

in which Christ joins His Word of promise to a __________________ __________________*;*

by which He offers and bestows the __________________ *of* __________ *He has earned for us by His suffering, death, and resurrection [also known as a Means of Grace].*

In **Baptism**, God links His Word to plain water and washes away our sins. In the **Sacrament of the Altar**, the Lord's Supper, God combines His Word of forgiveness with the bread and the wine, where Christ is truly present in His body and blood.

Read

Open your Small Catechism and read Question 296.

According to what you just read, why did Jesus institute the Sacraments?

Which Sacrament do you think is used to awaken faith? Why?

Which one is used to confirm faith? Why?

Reflect

Open your Small Catechism to Question 295, and read the answer and all the Bible passages.

Ever since you learned about Baptism in Unit 5, have you paid more attention to Baptisms in church? What things have you especially taken notice of?

Why do you think God "chose what is weak in the world to shame the strong" and ordinary things like bread and wine to do extraordinary works?

What gives a sacrament its power? Is it the element of water, bread, and wine, or is there something greater at work?

NOTES

NOTES

7.2 Where to Go?

As Jesus went into that Upper Room with His disciples to share with them His final meal, He knew that His time was almost up. That night, He would be betrayed, and the next day, He would go to the cross.

If you were in Jesus' shoes, that might seem pretty scary to know that you were going to the cross the next day. The upside for Jesus: knowing this was His final night with those He was closest to, He used that opportunity to invest in His disciples one final time.

If you had a chance to invest in your family and your friends one last time, what would you say to them? What would you pass on to them or leave for them to remember you by? Last will and testaments are things we don't think about until we're at the end of our lives. Only then do we typically take the time to plan what we'd like to say to those we love and share our final hopes.

As Jesus prepared for His final time together with His followers, He gathered them in an upper room in Jerusalem. He knew that this would be the last time that He would eat the Passover (a very important meal) with them.

This would be the most important meal He would have with them. It was here that Jesus would give to His disciples His last will and testament. It was here where He would share with them some of the most important things. It was at this meal that Jesus would **institute the Lord's Supper** as one final important parting gift for His disciples to share.

Read

MATTHEW 26:17–30

Number the events in the proper order.

____ Jesus and His disciples go out to the Mount of Olives.

____ Jesus reveals that Judas will betray Him.

____ The disciples make preparations for the Passover.

____ Jesus institutes the Lord's Supper.

NOTES

What words did Jesus say when instituting the Lord's Supper? Check out verses 26–29 if you need help. **Write them in the margin.**

How is this Sacrament connected with Jesus' death?

Jesus' institution of the Lord's Supper is contained in two other Gospels: **Mark 14:12–26** and **Luke 22:1–23**. **Take a moment to read through each account.** Notice how similar they are, but also note how they each include some different things. Each passage help us gain a bigger picture of what happened that night. **Now turn to 1 Corinthians 11:17–34 and read those verses.**

Here, the apostle Paul is correcting a church that had not been respectfully practicing the Lord's Supper. In fact, when the church came together, people were getting drunk on the wine, and some never even got to eat this sacred meal! Can you imagine people getting drunk on wine in church? Crazy, right?!

In verse 26, what does Paul say you do every time you take the Lord's Supper?

According to verse 27, what are you guilty of if you take the Lord's Supper in an unworthy manner?

Finally, in verse 28, what does Paul say you should do each time before taking the Lord's Supper?

NOTES

Reflect

This all sounds like serious business, and that's because it is. When we take the Lord's Supper, God desires us to have hearts ready to receive His grace. If we don't want His grace and forgiveness, or if we take it for granted or don't care about it, the apostle Paul says we can end up sinning against the very body and blood of Christ.

Don't worry, though! We'll learn more about how to receive the Lord's Supper properly later in this unit. For now, recognize that taking the Lord's Supper is important and not something to be taken lightly. God is delivering His grace as we receive His body and blood! It needs to be treated like the precious treasure it is.

How have you thought about the Lord's Supper in the past? Have you been more or less serious in your approach to it? Why?

Having read 1 Corinthians 11, how might you think of the Lord's Supper differently?

7.3 The Passover

Knowing that Jesus instituted the Sacrament of the Altar at this final meal, let's turn our attention to the important meal that Jesus was having with His disciples when He instituted this incredible gift. As we do, we'll see the incredible connections Jesus was making between what He was about to do and another great moment of God redeeming His people from slavery.

Jesus was sharing an important religious meal with His disciples called Passover, which connects back to the beginning of God's people Israel. The Passover meal is a celebration that God's people have been keeping for thousands of years because it commemorates one of the most critical events in the Bible: the exodus. Let's step back in time and dive into the Word to find out more about this significant event when **God took His people out of slavery and into freedom**.

Read

EXODUS 1:6–22

What has happened to the people of Israel while living in Egypt (v. 7)?

How does the pharaoh make it even worse for the Israelites (vv. 8–14)?

Look at Exodus 1:20. Has God forgotten or left the Israelites all on their own? Why did you answer as you did?

NOTES

While the Egyptian soldiers were hunting down Hebrew (Israelite) baby boys to throw them into the Nile river, one courageous mother risks everything to save her son. She hides him for as long as she can, and then places him in a basket and sends the basket down the river, where it is found by none other than Pharaoh's daughter. Realizing this is one of the baby boys that was supposed to be drowned in the river, she decides to rescue him, adopt him, and raise him as her own child! She names him Moses. He will come to be an essential person in God's plan of salvation.

- ☐ Moses becomes the **first great prophet of Israel**.
- ☐ He will **lead the people out of bondage and out of slavery**.
- ☐ He will take them through the desert wilderness and **lead them to the Promised Land**.

But to do all that, he would need God's help and power along the way. To free Israel from slavery, God sends ten plagues that impact the land and people of Egypt. Each plague comes and goes, but Pharaoh refuses to let God's people go until the tenth and final plague, the death of the firstborn sons and male animals. God sends this plague of death upon all firstborn sons who live in Egypt. That means it will affect even the sons born to Israelites. But hope is not lost! God provides a way to protect the Israelites and to commemorate the day.

This fateful night when God provided deliverance and a commemoration of the occasion is known as the Passover.

Read

EXODUS 12:1–13

How are the Israelites to protect their families from the plague of death upon the firstborn? **Fill in the blanks below with the instructions God gives Moses for the Israelites.**

First: Slaughter a ______________________.

Second: Place the ______________ on the doorposts.

Third: Eat the __________________ meal as you wait for the Lord to pass over your home.

Reflect

What do you think it was like to be a firstborn son living in Egypt when this tenth and final plague came?

Do you think it would be easy or hard to trust in the blood of the lamb on the doorpost to save your life? Why?

How easy do you find it to trust in Jesus to save your life? Why?

NOTES

NOTES

It's no secret: there is a tremendous significance to the connection between the first Passover and the Lord's Supper. You've now read through both events. This page is meant to help make some more connections between the two accounts to help you see God's incredible consistency in both of these monumental moments in history.

THE PASSOVER	THE LORD'S SUPPER
The people of Israel were slaves in Egypt.	We are slaves to sin.
God freely offered deliverance to His people.	"The free gift of God is eternal life in Christ Jesus our Lord." Romans 6:23
A lamb was sacrificed for the Passover.	"Behold, the Lamb of God, who takes away the sin of the world!" John 1:29
Those who believed and trusted God's Word were rescued.	Whoever hears the words of Jesus and believes in Him has eternal life.
The people of Israel were saved from the power of Pharaoh.	We are saved from the power of sin through the cross.
The people continued to celebrate the Passover, remembering God's grace.	"Do this in remembrance of Me." Luke 22:19; 1 Corinthians 11:24–25

THE PASSOVER LAMB	JESUS CHRIST
The Passover lamb was without blemish.	Jesus is without blemish.
The lamb was a male of the first year.	Jesus was the firstborn Son of God.
The lamb was set aside for four days on the tenth of the month of Nisan.	Jesus entered Jerusalem and was public for four days on the tenth of the month of Nisan.
The lamb was killed between the evenings at 3:00 p.m.	Jesus died at 3:00 p.m. (Mark 15:33–37)
The lamb's bones were not broken. (Exodus 12:46; Numbers 9:12)	Jesus' bones were not broken. (Psalm 34:20; John 19:31–32)
The blood of the lamb saved the Israelites' firstborn.	The blood of Christ saves us
The body of the lamb had to be eaten the same night.	Jesus was crucified, suffered, and died in the same night.
No work was to be done on the Passover; only the blood of the lamb could save.	The blood of Jesus, not our works, saves us. (1 Peter 1:18–21)

NOTES

7.4 In, With, and Under

Now that we know the biblical background for the Lord's Supper and the Passover, let's talk a little more about what we're participating in as we come to the Table for the Lord's Supper each week. **Turn to Question 349** in your Small Catechism.

Notice what it says Christ gives us in the Lord's Supper:

Christ gives us His own true body and blood for the forgiveness of sins.

At first, it might seem like crazy talk to say that when we eat the bread and drink the wine of the Lord's Supper, we are receiving the true body and true blood of Jesus. How is that possible?

Take a deep breath, and turn to Question 350 in your Small Catechism.

Find out a little more about why we believe and accept Jesus' words "This is My body" and "This is My blood" at face value.

As you read through the answer, **give the reasons why we accept Jesus' words in your own words** in the space below.

As we come to the Lord's Table, it's important for us to discern (that is, properly recognize) what it is that we're eating. As Jesus takes the bread, He says, "This is My body," and as He takes the cup of wine, He says, "This is My blood." So why do we believe that Christ's body and blood are present with the bread and the wine? Because that is exactly what Jesus said. As Jesus instituted the Lord's Supper, He mentions all four: bread, wine, body, and blood. We trust in Jesus' words as we come forward to receive this great mystery of His presence in this meal.

Read

JOHN 6:22–69

This is a long but important passage. Some of Jesus' followers during His earthly ministry also struggled with what it meant to eat Jesus' body as the bread of life. As you read this passage, **write down what you believe are the most important verses or words to remember** from this passage in the space below.

Turn to Question 352 in your Small Catechism.

Using what you read in the notes, write what the following words remind us of as we think about the Lord's Supper:

***In* reminds us . . .**

***With* reminds us . . .**

***Under* reminds us . . .**

Reflect

In the Bible, Jesus gives us many hard teachings. As we learned in our reading from John 6, the teaching that we receive His true body and blood is certainly one of those hard teachings.

Why do you think people would struggle to believe that we receive Jesus' true body and blood in the Lord's Supper?

Now think about your faith. Is it hard for you to believe and trust in the words of Jesus concerning the Lord's Supper? Why or why not?

NOTES

Other Views on the Lord's Supper

Since the Lord's Supper is a hard teaching from Jesus, not all Christians and churches agree on it. There are three different views of the Lord's Supper that you need to know to understand how specific churches believe different things about the Lord's Supper.

The information below gives us a simple way to see what everyone thinks about the Lord's Supper, including what it is and what we receive through it.

All this information can be reviewed by **looking at Question 360** in your Small Catechism.

Transubstantiation

This is the belief that the bread and wine transform into the body and blood of Christ when the words of Jesus are spoken.

You only receive the body and blood of Christ since the bread and wine have been transformed.

As a sacrament, forgiveness is received with the body and the blood.

This teaching is held by the Roman Catholic Church.

Symbolic

This is the belief that the bread and wine are symbols of the body and blood of Christ.

You only receive the bread and wine since they are only symbols.

As a symbolic meal, forgiveness is not received with the bread and wine.

This teaching is generally held by Baptist, Evangelical, and many nondenominational churches.

Real Presence

This is the belief that in, with, and under the bread and wine, we receive the body and blood of Christ because Jesus is really present in the meal.

You eat the bread and drink the wine and receive the true body and blood of Christ.

As a sacrament, forgiveness is received with the body and the blood.

This is the teaching of the Lutheran Church.

7.5 For You

Sometimes when everyone is going up to receive the Lord's Supper, it can seem like people are just getting in line because everyone else is. It can seem like sometimes people come to receive the Lord's Supper without really giving it much thought.

When you think about approaching the Lord's Table to receive His body and His blood, don't let that moment pass right by you. Remember the price paid and the gift that this meal is for us. Jesus died on the cross for the forgiveness of our sins. He has given us this meal as a means of continuing to pour out that forgiveness to us. If we simply go through the motions when we receive the Lord's Supper, we can miss one of the most critical pieces: **this meal—the true body and blood of Christ, along with His forgiveness—is for you.**

Think about it like this: at Christmastime, we all wonder which presents belong to which person. Is the big one mine? How about that little one? We know that each gift was chosen with a specific purpose in mind, so we want to make sure that each gift is given to the person whose name is on it—especially if it's our own. Your gift has your name on it for a reason: it's yours.

Jesus knew exactly what He was doing as He gave instructions to His disciples on how they were to carry out the Lord's Supper. He said, **"This is My body, which is given for you. . . . This is My blood, which is shed for you for the forgiveness of sins."**

You've likely heard these words spoken during the Divine Service. For example, see *LSB*, pages 162 and 164.

The Lord's Supper is a gift that comes with great benefits and power, and every time you receive it, you hear exactly for whom it is meant: you. Jesus wanted to make sure that you had no doubt about who He meant to give this gift of His body, blood, and forgiveness. He calls you by name each and every time.

Every time you go to the Lord's Table, you hear those words that remind you that this gift is specifically for you. As you hold out your hands, you'll hear, **"The true body of Christ, given for you. The true blood of Christ, shed for you."**

As you hear these words, go from the Table with no doubt of what has just happened. Jesus has delivered to you the gifts of His grace, His forgiveness, and Himself. He's addressed that gift directly to you so that you would have no doubt.

NOTES

As you walk away from the Table, Jesus wants you to know exactly who you are: a forgiven child of God for whom He died.

Turn to Question 362 in your Small Catechism.

As you read through the answers, **list the three benefits** that come from the Lord's Supper.

- ☐
- ☐
- ☐

Reflect

Would you ever reject a gift that someone gave to you? Why or why not?

Now that you know the benefits of the Lord's Supper and that they are there for you, would there ever be a reason why you would reject His gift in this meal?

NOTES

The reality is that sometimes you don't feel like this gift of the Lord's Supper, and its benefits, are for you. Sometimes, you feel like your sins are so big or bad that God could never forgive you. Other times, you feel like you haven't been faithful enough as a Christian to deserve this meal.

In the margin, describe a time when you felt like your sins were so wrong that God couldn't or wouldn't forgive you. If you don't want to be that candid, write a few words that would help remind you of what you're thinking about.

The good news is that God says His forgiveness is always there for you. That's a reminder He offers to us each and every time we come to the Lord's Table.

1 John 1:9 says,

> **If we confess our sins, He is faithful and just to forgive us our sins and to cleanse us from all unrighteousness.**

This gift of the Lord's Supper and His forgiveness is for you, and God invites you to come to His Altar to receive it.

NOTES

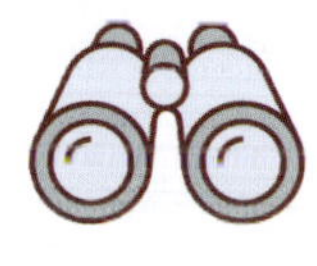

7.6 Examining Ourselves

You are almost done with Unit 7—only two more lessons to complete! But don't rush through, because this lesson is one of the most important. In this section, we're talking about how to prepare yourself to receive the Lord's Supper in a worthy manner. Whether you're preparing to receive Communion for the first time or you've been receiving it for a lifetime, these things are crucial for us to keep in mind as we approach the Table to receive the Lord's Supper.

Let's think about how you prepare for other things in your life. Write down a few ways that you get ready for the following activities:

Going on vacation:

Taking a big test:

Playing in a championship basketball game:

Getting ready for each of these activities requires you to do a few things. You can't just show up and expect that your vacation will be awesome when you haven't packed. You can't expect to just show up and think that you will pass your test when you haven't studied. You also can't just show up expecting to win the game when you haven't practiced. The same is true with the Lord's Supper.

There is a certain amount of "getting ready" or preparing yourself that the Bible requires when we come to participate in the Lord's Supper. What are some ways that you've seen your parents, family members, and others in church prepare to receive the Lord's Supper?

Read

Turn to Questions 367, 368, and 369 in your Small Catechism.

What do we need to have to receive the Lord's Supper worthily?

What can happen, or what are we guilty of, if we receive the Sacrament in an unworthy manner? (Be sure to look at 1 Corinthians 11:27–28.)

NOTES

Reflect

In 1 Corinthians 11:27–28, the apostle Paul makes it clear that if we are not well prepared, then we can eat and drink judgment upon ourselves. So, how do we prepare for it? We start by examining ourselves!

> How do I need to prepare myself physically? (See Question 370.)
>
> How do I examine myself? (See Question 371.)
>
> What if I'm struggling in my faith? Should I receive the Lord's Supper? (See Question 372.)

Examining yourself is like looking closely in a mirror. You can begin to see things that at first you didn't know were there. What do you think you would discover about yourself and the sins in your life if you stopped and examined yourself carefully as though looking in a mirror?

Below you'll find a list of practical ways to prepare yourself to receive the Lord's Supper. Check the box by at least three that you will do.

- ☐ I will pray, confess my sins, and ask God to forgive me.
- ☐ I will read through 1 Corinthians 11:23–28.
- ☐ I will commit to changing my life and living according to God's desires and His will for my life.
- ☐ I will declare my faith in Jesus, confirming that I trust Him with my whole life (past, present, and future).
- ☐ I will make an intentional effort to listen to or sing the worship music while I wait to go forward to receive the Lord's Supper.
- ☐ I will go to my family or friends and ask for forgiveness if I have hurt them or sinned against them.
- ☐ I will speak with a pastor about my faith, my sins, and my desire for forgiveness.
- ☐ I will fast on the days I know I will be taking Communion.

Scenario

You have just gotten out of the car when your brother smacks the back of your head and takes off running. You chase him down and toss him to the ground, ready to get him back. Right then, you feel the strong hands of your father grab you and lift you off your brother. In a stern voice, he yells at you for tackling your brother. Now, you're super angry at both your brother and your dad. As you walk into church, you take one more shot at your brother when Dad's not looking. You are smugly proud of yourself for getting away with payback.

Do you think you should receive the Lord's Supper that morning? Why or why not? (Look at Question 374 E. for clues.)

What could you do, right there in your church, to properly prepare for Communion?

7.7 A Life of Receiving

Imagine there was one place—one physical location in the entire world—you could go that would give God's promise of forgiveness, salvation, and life. Would you go there? Of course!

What would you be willing to do to make sure you got there? Probably just about anything. Would you climb a mountain? You bet! Cross over a valley on a rope bridge? Piece of cake. How often would you go? As often as possible.

That's what we do when we come to the Table to receive the Lord's Supper. We are given, and we receive, the forgiveness of sins, the salvation of our souls, and new life in Christ. It may seem simple to come and eat a small piece of bread and drink a small amount of wine. It may even seem foolish that doing such things could bring about forgiveness, salvation, and life. Even so, God's Word and promise delivers these to us as we take, eat, and drink the Lord's Supper.

Week after week in worship services, faithful disciples come to the Altar of the Lord and receive the bread and wine to eat and drink. Hopefully, by now, you've come to realize this is a vital act of faith for those who follow Jesus. It is something He commanded His disciples to do not only once but regularly.

Jesus knew that His followers would need ongoing support and strengthening of their faith, so He provided this meal. He also knew that a regular physical connection would be beneficial.

So we come to another one of our faith habits for the journey:

FAITH HABIT #6: RECEIVE THE LORD'S SUPPER.

Each time you come to receive the Lord's Supper is an opportunity for you to reflect on your need for forgiveness and to repent of your sins. This is why coming to the Table isn't just a one-time thing. **It's a lifelong habit!** It's a physical place where Jesus comes to you with His forgiveness. In response, you have an opportunity to give thanks to the Lord for the life and salvation He grants you through Jesus Christ. It is an opportunity to proclaim the Lord's death until He returns and to celebrate that Jesus, the Lamb of God, has taken away your sins.

NOTES

We receive this meal in remembrance of all that Jesus has done for us. We recall His life, ministry, death, and resurrection. Each time we receive the Lord's Supper, we are once again grounded in the foundation of Christ Jesus.

Read

MATTHEW 26:28

What comfort can the Lord's Supper offer you each time you receive it?

1 CORINTHIANS 11:23–26

What is it that we remember when we receive the Lord's Supper? When do you think it's important to remember these things?

Look at Question 363 in your Small Catechism.

What are the four reasons given for receiving this Sacrament frequently?

- ☐
- ☐
- ☐
- ☐

Which of these four do you think is the most compelling reason to receive the Sacrament frequently? Why?

NOTES

In the Large Catechism (an expanded version of the Small Catechism), Martin Luther notes how the Sacrament is "a pure, wholesome, comforting remedy that grants salvation and comfort. It will cure you and give you life both in soul and body. For where the soul has recovered, the body also is relieved" (Large Catechism, The Sacrament of the Altar).

God knew that it would be essential for us to connect with Him and interact with Him regularly. He gave us this Sacrament, the Lord's Supper, so that we could commune with Him, receive His grace and forgiveness, and have a tangible way to know that He is present with us. Each time we come to the Lord's Table, we have a chance to taste and see that the Lord is good!

Reflect

Think about a time when you went without food for a long time. What was it like to be super hungry?

Now consider what it would be like to go without being spiritually fed for a long time. How would it affect your faith?

What is it like when you see the congregation participating in the Lord's Supper? Or, if you already receive the Lord's Supper, what is it like for you? Describe what you see and experience, and even what you might be feeling.

NOTES

What did you have for breakfast this morning? What did you have for breakfast a week ago? Sometimes, it's hard to remember the little things that are routine, but it doesn't mean those things weren't meaningful. The Lord's Supper, when received frequently, can feel like a little thing, but it still has a significant impact on your faith. Many times, we have to make sure that we don't take for granted the gift that is the Lord's Supper.

What are some things you can do to prevent you from taking the Lord's Supper for granted?

In your own words, share why you would want to receive the Lord's Supper often.

Our lives as Christians are fueled by God's grace. He gives us that grace by means of the Sacraments and His Word. He commands us to receive this Sacrament often so that we might reap the benefits of His grace. Though we may not be able to receive the Lord's Supper every week, we should seek it out as often as it is available. After all, it is the very grace of God and His forgiveness given to you!

NOTES

FAQs about Communion

Your Small Catechism is full of some pretty incredible questions, answers, and Bible verses on this topic of the Lord's Supper. You might also have other practical questions when it comes to Communion. These two pages highlight a few of them. Have fun exploring your catechism for more questions, and be sure to ask a parent, mentor, or pastor if other questions arise.

Does everyone who receives Communion receive the body and blood in the Sacrament whether they believe or not? Great question! Yes, they do. Christ's Word, not our faith, establishes His presence in the meal. However, only through faith in Christ's words does one receive the blessings and benefits that are delivered as you receive this meal. For more information, check out Question 353 in your Small Catechism.

Should I take the common cup or an individual one? That's completely up to you. There's something beautiful in the picture Christ gives us of being able to take from one cup—we're not only united with Him but united with one another. Just as that cup of wine is made up of many grapes, so, too, is Christ's Body—His Church—made up of many members. Ultimately, the decision is up to you.

Is Jesus sacrificed again every time we take Communion? No, but that is the official view of the Roman Catholic Church. The body and blood of Jesus in the Sacrament are the complete sacrifice offered to God once for all on the cross. His body and His blood are now distributed to us in the Lord's Supper together with all the blessings and benefits that His sacrifice won for us. For more information, check out 1 Corinthians 5:7 and Hebrews 10:14, 17–18.

Will I get sick from taking from the common cup? All signs point to no. The common cup is actually a more sanitary approach to receiving Christ's blood. The alcohol in the wine, the antimicrobial activity of the silver of the cup, and the process of wiping it off with a fresh cloth largely reduce any risk at all. In other words, you're more likely to contract germs from the door handle leading into church or shaking someone's hand than from the common cup. Even so, if you are sick, it would be courteous of you to either receive last or choose an individual cup on that day.

Am I allowed to come forward if I'm weak or struggling in my faith? You bet! Question 372 tells us, "The words 'for you' show us that Christ instituted this Sacrament for weak and struggling sinners like us." Christ draws us near to Him in our brokenness so that He might strengthen our faith in Him, His promises, and the work He is doing in our lives. For more information, **read the verses that follow Question 372 in your Small Catechism**.

Should I receive Communion when I go to a church that I don't regularly attend? Great question! A good rule of thumb to go by is that your preference is always to take Communion at the church that you call home. In 1 Corinthians 4:1, God charges pastors with the responsibility of being stewards (or managers) of His mysteries, which includes the Sacrament of the Altar. With that, it's best to take Communion from someone you would call pastor—a spiritual authority in your life. If visiting another congregation of The Lutheran Church—Missouri Synod (LCMS), be sure to show up early and talk to a pastor before the service to make sure they aren't caught by surprise with a new face at the Communion Table. If not attending an LCMS congregation, it would be most appropriate for you to receive a blessing rather than participate in Communion.

Are we supposed to receive both the body and the blood each time we take Communion? Yes. Jesus' words invite us to receive both His body and His blood in the bread and the wine. To only receive one would be to dishonor what Christ invites us to do. For more information, check out Question 357 in your Small Catechism.

What advice do you have for me when I'm sitting in service and about to receive Communion? What should I be thinking about? Another great question! Here are some thoughts:

> As the pastor says them, listen to Jesus' words. You might even close your eyes to imagine the moment when Jesus spoke the words for the very first time. Just as He spoke them to His disciples, He is saying them to us as well.
>
> Be sure to examine yourself and pray before or even as you come forward. Have you acknowledged your sin? Have you truly taken the time to confess and be forgiven? As you come forward, you want to make sure you've laid everything before God so that you can receive full and free forgiveness for everything you've brought before Him.
>
> Remember to indicate that you'd like to receive by holding your hands out.
>
> When you return to your seat, it's a great opportunity for you to pray again, thanking God for the gift that He's just given you and asking Him to help you continue on the right path and turn from your sins.

NOTES

Unit 7 Reflection

Now that you've worked through this unit on the Lord's Supper, it's time to reflect a bit on it as a whole.

Talk to someone who has been taking Communion for a long time (a parent, grandparent, guardian, mentor, or pastor would be a great choice, but any follower of Jesus in your life will do). Ask this person the following questions and record his or her response.

Do you remember taking Communion for the first time? When and where was it? What do you remember about how you felt about it?

Why is regularly receiving Communion important in the life of a Christian?

How do you prepare to receive the Lord's Supper?

What do you cherish most about the Lord's Supper?

Taking It Home

NOTES

Time for you to reflect personally on the Lord's Supper:

What about the Lord's Supper is most important to you?

What do you think is the most important thing people should know about the Lord's Supper? Why?

Why is it important to believe in the real presence of Jesus' body and blood in, with, and under the bread and the wine in the Lord's Supper?

Why is it important to recognize that it is God's power at work through His Word in the Lord's Supper?

How has your understanding of Jesus' love for you changed or deepened after working through this unit?

Write a brief prayer in the space below that you could use every time you are preparing to receive the Lord's Supper or even after you have received it.

NOTES

You have completed Unit 7.

Complete your Unit Check-In.

NOTES

Unit 8

Continuing the Journey

NOTES

We began our time together at the start of this journal talking about this incredible journey we are on called life. Sometimes, life is thrilling; other times, it seems boring. Sometimes, it seems bleak and makes us afraid; other times, it brings us beauty and joy beyond what we could have ever imagined.

As we started this leg of the journey of life—the part we refer to as the confirmation journey—we acknowledged that as we go through life, we ask ourselves some pretty important questions along the way: What am I supposed to do with the time that I'm given for this journey? Will I make the most of this journey? Or will I rush through it and miss some of the best parts? Will I give up when the journey seems tough? Or keep pushing toward the end because I know it will be worth it?

This time together has been all about allowing you to engage with some of those big questions while we've asked some other important questions to guide us along the way: Who am I? Who is God? How do I live my life? How does God interact with me and how do I interact with Him? Hopefully, as you look back on your confirmation journey, you see it as one that was worth it, centering you around what God has always had in store for you.

For this final unit, it's time to look back so that you can gear up for what's next. Most likely, you will soon publicly confirm both your identity as a follower of Jesus and that the faith you have been given in your Baptism is what you know and confess to be true. This is a big moment for you, one worth celebrating.

But what is beyond confirmation? What's ahead of you? Life.

While that may seem a bit intimidating, here is some good news for you: this confirmation journey has prepared you well for what's next. Throughout this journal, you have slowly learned faith habits to take along with you as tools for the journey ahead. These habits foster and nurture faith as the Holy Spirit helps us all, as Christians, remain spiritually fit for the journey in front of us. This final unit will

revisit those habits as you consider how they will become a regular part of your life moving forward.

While the road ahead of you may not always be easy, rest assured in the final promise Jesus gave to His disciples:

> **And behold, I am with you always, to the end of the age.**
> **Matthew 28:20**

With those words, enjoy this final unit as you embrace what it might look like for these habits to serve as your guide as you **continue the journey**.

8.1 Request the Spirit

The very first faith habit for the journey that we discussed may have been a little intimidating when you first read it:

FAITH HABIT #1: REQUEST THE SPIRIT.

Now that you've grown in your understanding of God's work in your life, and especially the role of the Holy Spirit in our everyday lives as the Church, this has hopefully developed into an encouraging habit for you to consider again as you close your confirmation journey. The simple truth is this: we would be lost without the Spirit working in our lives. We're so thankful He does!

What now? How might this habit take shape in your life once this confirmation journey has concluded?

As we introduced this habit, we considered at least a few places where this habit will take shape naturally: when we engage God's Word and as we gather together with God's people for worship. Requesting the Spirit in these times helps us focus on what God has done as He drowns out our distractions.

But how might this extend into other parts of your life moving forward?

In Unit 3, you learned all about the Holy Spirit and the incredible things He does. The Holy Spirit is **a life-giver**, **a gift-giver**, and **a fruit-producer**, who works within and **gathers the Church** (God's people) **into communion** (fellowship) with one another to **nurture and strengthen our faith through the Word of God**, where we also receive **forgiveness** and the gift of **faith**, which leads to **eternal life** that will follow the coming **resurrection** of all who have died in the faith. In short: the Holy Spirit is capable of so many incredible things. Where else might the Holy Spirit extend in your life? At school? At home? With friends? The possibilities are endless.

NOTES

What does this look like? How does one request the Holy Spirit? By taking a moment to offer God a prayer as simple as this:

Go ahead and take a moment to pray this out loud! Practicing out loud will help this become a habit for your life.

Holy Spirit, be with me. Guide me. I need You. Set me apart. In Jesus' name. Amen.

Augustine of Hippo has long been considered one of the most important Early Church Fathers, leaders of the Church as it was taking shape in the world following Jesus' resurrection. He was born about three hundred years after Jesus poured out His Spirit on the apostles at Pentecost and began the Church.

Augustine suggested that rather than praying for what we need, we should pray to increase our desire for God so that we would better receive what He is preparing to give us. Why? Because God already knows what we need before we ask! With this in mind, he wrote this prayer **requesting the Holy Spirit**:

Pray this one out loud too! Take a moment to pause and breathe before you pray so that you can focus in this moment and let these words become a sincere prayer from you.

Breathe in me, O Holy Spirit, that my thoughts may all be holy.

Act in me, O Holy Spirit, that my work, too, may be holy.

Draw my heart, O Holy Spirit, that I love but what is holy.

Strengthen me, O Holy Spirit, to defend all that is holy.

Guard me, then, O Holy Spirit, that I always may be holy. Amen.

As you consider these words, remember what the word *holy* means: set apart. As you look forward to what God has in store for you beyond confirmation, keep in mind that He has **set you apart** in your Baptism. He has made you holy by placing in you the Holy Spirit.

What does this mean? God's intention for your life is that every piece of you would be holy: your thoughts, your words, your actions, your decisions, your desires—every piece of who you are as you live your life.

As you look ahead, will you be perfect at being holy and set apart in every aspect of your life? Absolutely not. You're going to mess up. We all do! But you do have help that was given to you in your Baptism: the Holy Spirit. He goes with you and, through prayers like the ones mentioned on page 268, you will continue to see His work more clearly in your life as this becomes a habit in your life.

In St. Augustine's prayer, circle the parts that you find most meaningful to you. Why do you find those parts meaningful?

In what part of your life do you feel like you could use this prayer the most: at home, in school, in church, with friends, in your neighborhood? Why?

NOTES

NOTES

8.2 Read and Repeat

As we started this confirmation journey together, our very first unit focused on God's Word and how important it is for our lives. God's Word, through the Holy Spirit, points us to Jesus, works within us both Law and Gospel, and gives us this gift called faith, which leads to eternal life! **God's Word creates, it gives life, and it brings restoration to broken lives.** Nothing else in all creation can do what God's Word is capable of doing. God's Word is powerful, and He continues to work through His Word as He promised.

As we reflect on both our journey together and as we look to God's journey with His people throughout history, we see how time in God's Word is crucial for us as Christians. It's not optional; it's necessary.

With that reality, we came to our second faith habit for the journey:

FAITH HABIT #2: READ AND REPEAT THE WORD OF GOD.

Engaging God's Word on a regular basis helps you to grow in, sustain, and live out the faith that was given to you in your Baptism. Like water to a plant, God's Word nurtures faith in a way that nothing else can.

So when you look at the journey ahead of you, how might your commitment to God's Word also go with you after you confirm your faith publicly?

Here are some potential starting steps as you consider this question:

- ☐ **Make a commitment.** In order to make something a habit or make a change, you need to make a personal commitment. There's no better time than the present to make God's Word a regular part of your life.
- ☐ **Tell others about your commitment.** When you tell others, it helps to keep you accountable. It invites them to ask you how it's going. If you keep that commitment just between you and God, it's easier to slip up. Share it!
- ☐ **Start small and stay committed.** Even if your commitment is only to set a timer and read for five minutes each day, that's a start—it's a great start! Make sure you don't let anything knock you off track. Be absolutely determined to make this a permanent habit in your life, especially in the first few months. If you start skipping days, it will be much harder to stay committed to this new habit.
- ☐ **Go with others.** Ask your family if they'd be open to making it a family habit. Ask a friend! When we bring people along with us, we're living out God's intentions for us in our lives. God brings us together for a reason.

Above all, consider this: where is some place that you can always guarantee that God's Word will be read and talked about? Church. When we gather together as God's people, as the Church, we gather around God's Word and His Sacraments. That's what worship is by definition! Worship is an opportunity for us, as God's people, to be fed by Him. So one more great way to make sure this commitment continues with you after you confirm your faith is by making worship a nonnegotiable for your life. Allow God's Word to be a priority for you and your life, and you will find this faith that you are confirming will continue to grow and mature.

NOTES

NOTES

Reflect

Why will it be important for you to make God's Word a priority for your life beyond confirmation? Consider how it has helped you in the past.

What do you think will be the biggest challenges to engaging with God's Word as a regular part of your life beyond confirmation?

What questions do you have about this habit that will help you get started with making this commitment beyond confirmation?

8.3 Resist the Ancient Enemies

In Unit 4, you explored what it means to daily receive God's gifts and commend your life to His care through the words of the Lord's Prayer. In that same conversation, you were introduced to our third faith habit for the journey:

FAITH HABIT #3: RESIST THE ANCIENT ENEMIES.

For the most part, we tend to get along with the people in our lives. We don't really consider ourselves as having many enemies. Sure, we have disagreements at times and we certainly have our rivals in times of competition. But enemies? Likely not. To many of us, the idea of having enemies can seem like a foreign concept.

Yet, as you learned what it means to pray "lead us not into temptation" and as you explored this habit, we clearly identified three ancient enemies:

The Devil, the World, and Our Sinful Flesh

As you come to the conclusion of this confirmation journey and look forward to the road ahead, it will be critical for you to become more aware of the temptations these enemies will use to challenge you and your faith. Each one of these enemies has one desire: to pull you away from Jesus. Why? Because in Jesus, you have life and life in abundance.

As you use this lesson to reflect on the challenges that could come your way, know this as well: the King of Life fights for you every step of the way. As Jesus said to the Eleven before He ascended:

> **I am with you always, to the end of the age. Matthew 28:20**

God will not abandon you in your challenges, and He will not leave you by yourself when these temptations come your way. He will always be with you! You are never alone.

NOTES

Reflect

Which of the three ancient enemies do you think is the hardest to resist: the devil, the world, or your sinful flesh? Why?

Remember the devil's only weapon is a lie. What's the best way you have found to combat a lie?

Think ahead to the next five years of your life. What do you imagine will be the most tempting thing the world will throw your way in that time? Why do you think that will be the hardest thing to resist?

NOTES

When you think about your sinful flesh, there's a strong chance you find yourself going back to the same sin over and over. It's true for us all. A great step to take when you find yourself trapped in the same habit is to share with a trusted adult in your life to receive some guidance on how to break that cycle. This would be a faithful guardian or mentor who wants the best for you. Who comes to mind when you think of that kind of trusted adult? Why?

In sports, it can be helpful to study your opponent to learn what kind of plays they may run against you. The same can be said for these ancient enemies. How do you plan to resist them? What are some specific and intentional things you could do that will help you resist their temptations?

NOTES

8.4 Remember Your Baptism

As you entered into Unit 5 of this journey, you began to explore a two-part question at length: How do I interact with God and how does God interact with me? As we unpacked that question, we learned that God's primary way of interacting with us is through the Means of Grace, which are the Sacraments and His Word. With each of the Means of Grace also came a faith habit for the journey.

As we explored how God interacts with us and how we interact with God in Baptism, we learned our fourth faith habit for the journey:

FAITH HABIT #4: REMEMBER YOUR BAPTISM.

The practice of remembering your Baptism will be a central one for you to embrace every single day moving forward in the journey ahead. In Baptism, God claimed you as His own. You were brought into the family and can proudly say that you are a child of God! You were united with Jesus' death and resurrection. You were given faith! And who did all of this? God did it all through His Word combined with the waters that were poured over you. You were simply a gracious recipient on the other end of that baptismal promise.

So why is it so important to remember your Baptism? Why is it important to remember this promise that was given to you? Because doubts will come. Your faith will be challenged and tested. And what's the most important thing you can do when those times come? Turn back to God and His promises to hear what He has to say and be reminded of what He has already taken care of.

God, the King of the Universe, has already taken care of your salvation in Jesus Christ. Almighty God, in His mercy, has already given faith to you in the waters of Baptism. It was His Word—not yours—that mattered most at your Baptism. His Word creates. His Word gives life. Your word and mine? Not so much.

Every single day is a great day to remind yourself of the promises that are yours because of what God has done in your life, especially in the waters of Baptism. No matter what challenges or doubts the devil and the world will throw your way, you can always point back to your Baptism, where God did all the work and you were on the receiving end of some incredible promises.

Reflect

Imagine one of your friends says to you tomorrow, “My grandma really wants me to get baptized, but I’m not really sure I understand why that’s so important for her. What do you think?” How would you respond? Be sure to share reasons why you think your Baptism is important to you.

Every time someone gets baptized at church, it can be a great reminder of the same promise that was given to you in your Baptism. Think about the last time you witnessed someone get baptized. What were some of the things that happened or words that were spoken that stuck out to you? Write down as many as you can.

When you remember your Baptism, you are reminded that God has already taken care of your salvation, bringing you a deep sense of peace. On a scale of 1 to 10 (1 being completely anxious and 10 being completely at peace), how peaceful do you feel about your salvation? Why did you choose that number?

8.5 Repent and Be Forgiven

As you explored the practice of Confession and Absolution, Unit 6 continued investigating both sides of the question "How do I interact with God and how does He interact with me?" It's there you were introduced to your fifth faith habit for the journey.

FAITH HABIT #5: REPENT AND BE FORGIVEN.

Like remembering your Baptism, repentance is meant to be a habit you exercise every single day, and it can be an incredibly helpful one as you navigate and own each of your mistakes.

As you learned in Unit 6, we've all fallen short of the glory of God. Not one of us is perfect, and that includes you. We fall short of His glory every single day. As much as we may try, we'll never have a perfectly sinless day until Jesus returns. That's why God gave us this invitation to turn to Him in repentance and receive what He alone can give: **forgiveness**.

As you grow, you'll learn that forgiveness can be a rare thing for people to find in this world. People can be cruel to one another and demand justice much faster than they offer forgiveness to others for their mistakes. But it doesn't have to be this way! God calls His Church, His people, to be a light in this world of darkness—to let His light shine before all people. You can shine that light for others to see! One of the best ways you can bear witness to the love God has for the people in your life is by boldly and freely embracing this faith habit for the journey.

When you openly admit that you've made mistakes and seek forgiveness from the people your mistakes have affected and from God, you're showing that forgiveness is possible. Will it always be easy? Not a chance. But it will be powerful!

When the time comes that you need some courage to remember how important repentance can be, look to Jesus. There on the cross, He reminds you how far He is willing to go so you can be free of your sin. Every day you will have the opportunity to turn to Him, turn away from your sin, and receive His forgiveness so you can rise up and walk in the newness of life that He has in store for you.

Reflect

What do you think will be your greatest challenge to embracing this habit of repenting and being forgiven: what other people think about your mistakes or how you feel about your mistakes?

Imagine you're talking to a friend who agrees with your answer above. They share with you that either other people's thoughts about their mistakes or their own feelings about their mistakes are keeping them from repenting and being forgiven. What words would you share with them to encourage them to repent and receive the forgiveness that God promises them?

When the time comes for you to repent, a great practice is to share with someone out loud that you've made a mistake. A trusted adult is a great place to get some practice with this. This could potentially be someone in your family or a mentor.

Who would be someone with whom you could practice what it means to share out loud when you've made a mistake?

Feel free to name multiple people! Refer back to this list the next time you make a mistake so you can start practicing what it means to repent.

What about this person makes you feel like they would be a great person with whom to share a confession?

NOTES

8.6 Receive the Lord's Supper

In our final unit wrestling with the question "How do I interact with God and how does He interact with me?" we navigated what it means that God comes to us in the Sacrament of the Altar. It's here you learned the sixth faith habit for the journey:

FAITH HABIT #6: RECEIVE THE LORD'S SUPPER.

Like Baptism, the Lord's Supper can seem pretty simple to an outsider. It's just simple bread and a little wine, right? What's the big deal? As you learned in Unit 7, the big deal is that your Savior chooses to come to you over and over again in, with, and under that bread and wine through His body and His blood to give you His forgiveness.

Your God knows you well! He knows, as we've already discussed in this unit, that doubts will come your way. He knows the devil will do his best to convince you that somehow God's promises aren't for you. That's why the gift you receive in Holy Communion can be such a valuable one to receive as often as you are able.

Jesus invites you to His Table just as you are, every single time. He does not require you to clean yourself up to come to receive His gifts. He only calls you to acknowledge, recognize, and respect who He is and the gift He is passing to you in the Holy Meal. It's His Table. It's His invitation. And it's you that He invites to receive.

When you find yourself feeling distant or too far gone, He draws you near to Himself and gives you His own body and blood for the forgiveness of all of your sins. Every time you step away from His Table having received what He alone gives you there, you go with His peace, His promise, and His presence, renewed by the forgiveness you have received from Him alone.

This is why we make it a regular practice to gather together as the Church and do not give up meeting together as some are in the habit of doing (see Hebrews 10:25). As we come together as the Body of Christ, we receive His gifts with thanksgiving and praise, renewed and energized for the journey He places before us. The assurance He gives us in the Lord's Supper helps us to take up that journey with freedom and confidence.

Reflect

Look up how often your church celebrates Communion as a congregation each month. Write the regular schedule for the service(s) you attend in the space below.

What do you think will be the biggest roadblock to regularly receiving the Lord's Supper as often as you are able?

Talk with your parent or guardian about the roadblock you see coming. Discuss ways you might be able to remove that potential roadblock, and write them down in the space below.

What is your biggest motivation for making the Lord's Supper a regular habit in your life in the years ahead? In your own words, why will receiving the Lord's Supper be so important specifically for you?

NOTES

NOTES

8.7 Remain in His Love

Open up your Bible or Bible app and **read or listen to John 15:1–17**.

It's time to introduce your final faith habit for the journey. That's right!

FAITH HABIT #7: REMAIN IN HIS LOVE.

This passage from John 15 is one of the final teachings Jesus gives to His disciples before He heads to the Garden of Gethsemane to be betrayed the night before He was crucified. A teacher might often save some of the most important lessons until the very end. That's certainly the case for Jesus here.

Jesus uses the word ***abide*** (or, in other translations, "remain") eleven times in those seventeen verses from John 15. He's trying to bring home a point to His disciples. Not only is this one of His final lessons, but any time we see Jesus repeat Himself, it means that He really wants us to understand and take to heart what He's saying. And what's at the heart of this final lesson to His disciples?

> **As the Father has loved Me, so have I loved you. Abide in My love. If you keep My commandments, you will abide in My love, just as I have kept My Father's commandments and abide in His love.**
> **John 15:9–10**

As you conclude this confirmation journey, the journey of life continues well into the years ahead for you. The question you have to ask yourself is this:

> **In the years ahead, will I still be remaining in God's love for me?**

God has made His love for you known. He is willing to step into time, to take on flesh, to go to the cross, to carry the sin of the world, and to rise from the dead so that nothing in all of creation would be able to separate you from Him. And at the same time, He will not force you to remain in His love; He only invites you into it. He places opportunities in front of you to interact with Him every single day, but He won't force you to partake of those opportunities.

That's one of the most interesting things about our God. He doesn't make us robots. While His Word creates faith in us and brings us to life when we cannot save ourselves or ask for help because we're spiritually dead due to our sin, we are also given the freedom to refuse His gifts and promises, choosing eternal separation from Him rather than receiving His gift of faith, which leads to eternal life.

In the journey ahead, the choice will be yours whether to remain in the faith God gave to you in your Baptism or to reject it—to remain in His love, as He calls you to do in John 15, or to cut yourself off like a vine separated from a tree.

As you consider this final faith habit for the journey, consider every invitation God is placing in front of you to remain in His love. What will your faith journey look like from this moment forward? Will it be filled with prayer? filled with conversations with fellow believers about the love God has for you? filled with time spent in His Word? Will it look like using the talents God has given you to bless others?

Jesus has extended and continues to extend His invitation to you every day to remain connected to Him and to one another. It's an invitation to remain in His love and an invitation we share in together as brothers and sisters in Christ. As you continue in this journey of learning what it means to seek, trust, and follow Jesus, know that you are not alone. We go together, and Jesus leads the way.

Reflect

Consider all the faith habits for the journey that you think would apply, as well as other habits or practices you think will be important, for you to remain intentionally in God's love. Be specific about what "remaining in God's love" will look like for you.

Take a second look at John 15:1–17. What part stands out to you the most? Why? **Write it in the margin.**

NOTES

8.8 Looking Back, Looking Forward

Welcome to the final lesson of your confirmation journey! Congratulations on a job well done! You've read, reflected, and responded to scenarios. You've spent time in God's Word, in the Small Catechism, and in conversations with people who have followed Jesus for a while. You made it! So now what?

This final lesson is an opportunity for you to consider what you're taking with you for the journey ahead. This is one final opportunity for you to reflect before you publicly confirm your baptismal faith before God and His people. And how will you do this? By writing a letter to yourself in the future.

Use the remaining pages of this journal to write to your future self. As you do, consider the following questions:

- ☐ What did you learn on this confirmation journey?
- ☐ Are you closer to God than you were before?
- ☐ Are you more aware of God's incredible love for you?
- ☐ Do you love God more than you did at the beginning of this journey?
- ☐ Are you different than you were when you began this journey?
- ☐ Do you see the world differently?
- ☐ Do you see your relationships with other people differently?
- ☐ Is your relationship with God different? How?

In a short time, you'll stand before God to publicly confirm your faith. You will be sharing with God and the world that the faith God has given to you in your Baptism is yours. You are claiming it for yourself.

The journey that follows is in your hands. How will this confirmation journey impact your day-to-day life moving forward? Will this be just a moment in time? Or will it be a catalyst for a lifelong journey of trusting and following Jesus with all that you have been given?

NOTES

NOTES

Dear ______________,

NOTES

NOTES